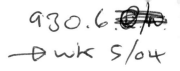

English ♯ Heritage
Book of
Shrines & Sacrifice

English ▦ Heritage
Book of
Shrines & Sacrifice

Ann Woodward

B.T. Batsford Ltd/English Heritage
London

© Ann Woodward 1992

First published 1992

All rights reserved. No part of this publication
may be reproduced, in any form or by any means,
without permission from the Publisher

Typeset by Lasertext Ltd, Stretford,
Manchester M32 0JT
and printed in Great Britain by
The Bath Press, Avon

Published by B. T. Batsford Ltd
4 Fitzhardinge Street, London W1H 0AH

A CIP catalogue record for this book is
available from the British Library

ISBN 0 7134 6080 6 (cased)
6084 9 (limp)

Contents

Illustrations

Colour plates

Acknowledgements

This book owes its being to the directors and sponsors of the excavations discussed within it. The results of these excavations have stimulated an ongoing debate concerning the nature of ancient religion and the beginnings of Christianity in Britain. My personal interest in this debate has been sharpened by involvement in two major projects: the preparation of the results of my own excavation at Uley for publication (for the Western Archaeological Trust and the Birmingham University Field Archaeology Unit), and formulation of a preliminary discussion of the results of the extensive excavation of the Roman cemetery at Poundbury, directed by Christopher Sparey Green (for the Dorchester Excavation Committee and Wessex Archaeology); both these projects were largely funded by English Heritage. Much reference will be made to the outstanding results obtained at Uley between 1976 and 1979, and I am particularly grateful to the landowners, Major and Mrs C. A. Goldingham, for permission to excavate, and to all members of the team who have contributed to the project over a period of fifteen years. For discussion of the Uley results, and for information concerning their own excavations, I am especially indebted to Christopher Sparey Green, Philip Rahtz and Warwick Rodwell. The structure and content of the book has been modified and improved with the assistance of Philip Rahtz, Peter Woodward, Stephen Johnson, and, at Batsford, Peter Kemmis Betty and Sarah Vernon-Hunt.

Friends and colleagues have been most generous in the provision of illustrations, or the granting of permission to reproduce illustrations from elsewhere, as follows: Mick Aston: 86, 93 and colour plate 9; Joe Bettey: 89; John Collis: 45; Philip Crummy: 79; Barry Cunliffe and Peter Davenport: 23; Martin Heard: 80; Anthony King and Grahame Soffe: 10, 20, 21, 22; Peter Leach: 5, 6, 66, 70, 88, 95 and colour plate 6; Roger Leech and the Society for Roman Studies: 43, 48, 54; Philip Rahtz: 3, 4, 34, 41, 69, 87; Joanna Richards: 26, 28, 75, 84 and colour plate 3 and front cover; Warwick Rodwell: 85; Christopher Sparey Green and Wessex Archaeology: 62, 63, 67, 68, 71, 78; Bryn Walters and the Roman Research Trust: 77. Colour plates 8 and 10 are reproduced by courtesy of the British Museum; colour plate 5 by courtesy of the Natural History Museum, Leo Biek and Christopher Sparey Green; illustration 92 by courtesy of the National Museums of Scotland; 40 and 51 by kind permission of The Trustees of the Clayton Collection; colour plate 1 and back cover are by J. E. Hancock; 65 and 73 are reproduced from Giles Clarke's *Winchester Studies 3*: Part II, *The Roman Cemetery at Lankhills* (1979), by permission of Oxford University Press; 24 and 27 are reproduced from *Temples in Roman Britain* by M. J. T. Lewis, by permission of Cambridge University Press; 13, 25, 39, 60 and 81 are reproduced from Research Reports IX and XL, by kind permission of the Society of Antiquaries of London.

Illustrations relating to the site of Uley are by Susan Banks (57), Mark Hassall (56), Helen Humphries (46); Gordon Kelsey (37, 38, 42, 47, 49 and 59), Peter Leach (colour plate 7), Trevor Pearson (11, 18, 19, 29, 30, 31, 74, 76, 82 and 83), Sebastian Rahtz (colour plates 2 and 4) and Joanna Richards (52, 53 and 55). Illustrations prepared specially for this book were drawn up by Dawn Flower at English Heritage (1, 2, 9, 44, 50, 58, 61, 72 and 73) and Peter Woodward (12, 14, 15, 16, 32, 33, 35, 36, 90 and 91). For photographic work throughout I am grateful to Graham Norrie, University of Birmingham. The text was skilfully processed by Ann Humphries.

1
Introduction

This book provides an analysis of Iron Age and Roman religious sites in Britain. It concentrates on the evidence for the special buildings, shrines, and for the various objects, alive, dead or symbolic, which were offered up as sacrifices within them. But first perhaps some definitions are necessary. In the contemporary western world a special religious building would most probably call to mind a church, or possibly a mosque or synagogue. Churches are by definition the centres for Christian worship, so in pre-Christian and other pagan contexts a different term is required. The most well-known word for a pagan religious building is temple. This has particular connotations, namely within the ancient Greek and Roman worlds, for the former centre of Jewish worship at Jerusalem and in certain sectors of the modern non-conformist Christian church. In spite of this, temple does seem to be a useful term for a religious building possessing some classical pretensions within the Roman world, and it will be used as such in the following chapters. But to define religious structures which are of any date, and of any persuasion, I have chosen the term shrine. In Christian usage, the word shrine is normally taken to be the altar, tomb or small chapel dedicated to the memory of a particular holy person, a saint, or may even be applied to the small casket containing the sacred relics of such a person. However, in archaeological and anthropological writing, a shrine has a wider meaning, and is taken to imply any building, although usually small in size, which was designed for ritual purposes.

The word sacrifice is another term which in modern usage possesses a restricted meaning, but can be employed at various levels. Primarily the word refers to the slaughter of a living body, whether animal or human, in a pagan religious context. Such actions will be referred to in the following analysis, but more space will be devoted to the analysis of inanimate sacrifices – the material items offered up to deities in shrines or graves, and also the ritual actions and verbal offerings, prayers and other utterances of propitiation or thanksgiving, which no longer exist. The ultimate abstract manifestation of the concept of sacrifice occurs in Christian theology, where acts of animal sacrifice were strictly forbidden. The crucifixion of Christ is viewed as the supreme sacrifice, and this event is regularly commemorated by the sacrifice of the Eucharist. Within this sacrament – 'the outward and visible sign of an inward and spiritual grace' – the ultimate sacrifice is re-enacted by the symbolic offering of the body and blood of Christ, and one's own self is also offered in a 'sacrifice of praise'.

This book is not a general study, of which several already exist, but is an analysis of what can be learned from the results of an impressive series of excavations that have taken place in Britain since the 1930s. Renewed interest in the subjects of Iron Age and Roman religions has been fired to a large extent by the results of these excavation campaigns and a number of books and reports have been published. None of these, however, has considered fully the aspects of continuity, and discontinuity, between the beliefs and religious activities of the Celtic, Roman and immediately post-Roman periods, and this will form a major theme running through the study presented here.

Forty years ago it was felt by some leading prehistorians that archaeological evidence could be used to reconstruct past systems of agricultural production, exchange of goods, social structure and political organization with some certainty. However, the realms of religious belief, or ideology as anthropologists would choose to say, were thought to be beyond the powers of archaeological interpretation. With the growth in data collection since then, and the development of more powerful frameworks of interpretation, archaeologists have become more daring. Indeed, much modern prehistoric research is concentrating on the ritual or ideological actions embedded within the apparently mundane activities of ancient everyday life. This book, however, will concentrate on the aspects of ideological activity that were special. These were special in that they were selective: particular actions were reserved for a prescribed time of the day, week or month or for festival days that occurred only once a year. They were enacted in specially

selected locations, where specific buildings or monuments had been constructed, and they were devoted to the veneration of a superhuman controlling power, usually conceived as a deity in human, animal or other natural form. Thus religion is a concept revealed by actions and these actions may be detected in the archaeological record in various ways. The most common forms of evidence relating to religion include special buildings and enclosures, monuments, the particular way a dead body was treated, material offerings found in or near special structures, and the contemporary reference to individual deities displayed in art (iconography), or the written word (inscriptions).

The sites

The bulk of the raw material used here comes from the results of 32 excavations, listed in the Appendix. This list is not exhaustive, but includes major sites where full reports are already in print, as well as those not yet

1 *The distribution of religious sites described in the text.*

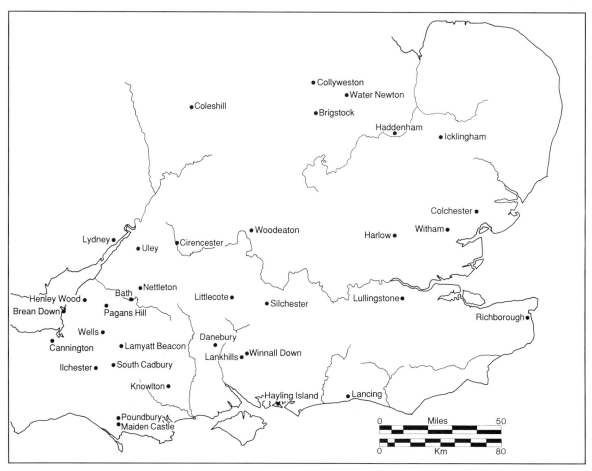

published where information has been supplied by their authors. The distribution of these sites, and some of the others mentioned in the book, is shown in (1). The concentration of sites in southern England reflects the overall distributions of Iron Age shrines and Roman temples. The large number of sites in the west is indicative of the fact that temples seem to have flourished in this zone during the late Roman period; also the publication of rural temple sites in this area seems to have outstripped the presentation of final reports on religious sites excavated in Roman towns, a type of settlement that was concentrated more in the south and east of the Roman province. Detailed discussion of the many structures, burials and objects found and recorded on the 32 sites selected for analysis will be included throughout the book in relation to the various periods and themes under consideration.

Evidence has been collected from sites of very differing form and character, many of them better known for their non-religious aspects. For instance, the plans of important shrines have turned up during the major excavation of some of our more famous hillforts, such as Danebury and South Cadbury, whilst many of the recently investigated temples lie inside, or just outside, other large hillforts in the south. Maiden Castle and Uley are notable examples. Other temples lay within Roman towns, such as Bath, and several of our late Roman Christian churches have also been found in urban situations. Other sites are located on isolated hilltops, or in the base of hidden valleys, close to sacred waters. In addition to structures provided for worship, this book will also be looking at some burial sites. From early Christian times these have been traditionally situated adjacent to and around the religious buildings themselves. However, in the Iron Age and Roman periods this generally was not so, and burials were often deposited within or on the margins of occupation sites. In the Roman period this is best illustrated by the occurrence of major cemeteries located just outside the walls of towns, as at Poundbury, west of Dorchester in Dorset, and at Lankhills outside the north gate of Roman Winchester.

The excavations

It is interesting to consider how the occurrence of excavations of such sites has changed and increased as the twentieth century has progressed (2). The campaigns before the Second World War were all masterminded by Sir Mortimer Wheeler, who not only established a systematic and scientific approach to archaeological recording, but also laid the foundations for many of the areas of Roman temple research that flourish today. The 1950s saw a widespread interest in temple excavation which took place from Somerset to Northamptonshire, but mainly as research exercises (3). In the 1960s some of the major rescue operations on temple sites were initiated, but the decade must be seen primarily as the era of late Roman cemetery excavations. A sudden realization that the excavation and study of rows and rows of apparently featureless, and findless, human burials could provide a great deal of evidence concerning late Roman ritual and the human population, linked to a gradual increase in funding for rescue archaeology, led to the instigation of the important cemetery excavations at Lankhills (Winchester), Poundbury and Cannington (4). Also to the late 1960s belonged the remarkable campaign of open-area excavation inside the Iron Age hillfort at South Cadbury. This turned up fine evidence for Iron Age shrines and associated animal sacrifices and, in terms of both conception and execution, was a good five years ahead of its time. By the 1970s modern rescue archaeology was well established and the following twenty years has seen the excavation of a highly varied group of Roman temples and cemeteries threatened with destruction by industrial or urban development, ploughing or treasure hunters. These include the excavation programmes carried out at Bath, Hayling Island, Harlow, Coleshill (5), Lamyatt, Shepton Mallet (6) and Uley. This time period has also seen the growth of large-scale investigation on Iron Age sites, both hillforts, such as Danebury, and on many settlement sites where important evidence for burial practices has been recovered.

Whilst in the pre-war period most excavations were funded by local donations and grants from academic bodies, the more extensive, and therefore more expensive, campaigns of the last three decades have often been funded by central government, firstly through the Ministry of Public Buildings and Works, then the Department of the Environment and now by English Heritage. Of the excavations listed in the Appendix, 58 per cent were funded by such

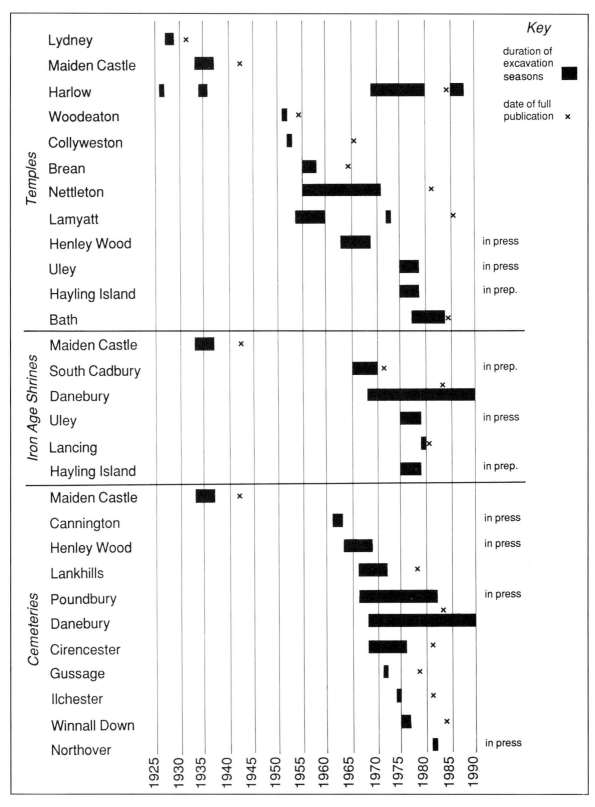

central grants, and of those projects initiated after 1970, 83 per cent have been funded in this manner. Government grants have been made available for shrines and temples slightly more often than for cemetery and church excavations. The type of excavation director has also changed through time with professional 'rescue unit' archaeologists gradually taking over from academics and unpaid enthusiasts. Of the sites listed in the Appendix, 52 per cent have been investigated by professional unit directors, 30 per cent by eminent academics, mainly from the university sector, and 18 per cent by unpaid enthusiasts. The last group includes amateur archaeologists and various other categories such as museum curators who undertake field projects during their holidays.

Archaeology is not primarily about exotic

2 *(Left) The main shrines and cemeteries: dates of excavation and publication.*

3 *(Right) Philip Rahtz emptying the temple well at Pagan's Hill, 1952.*

4 *(Below) Cannington: the excavation of a cemetery on the brink of a stone quarry.*

objects; it is more concerned with the reconstruction of all aspects of life in the past. Sometimes a find of exceptional importance is made, but the context of such finds is usually even more important than the intrinsic information offered by the object itself. Thus the greatest significance of the finding of fragments of the cult statue of Mercury at Uley (**7** and **colour plate 2**) was not only its artistic value but the fact that it had been dismembered. Selected pieces of it had subsequently been deposited in chosen places under the buildings constructed on top of the demolished Roman temple (see p. 118). Similarly, the importance of the Shepton Mallet chi-rho pendant (**colour plate 6**) lies not only in its unique construction but in the fact that it is the first Christian object to have been found sealed within the filling of a late Roman grave in Britain.

The concept of continuity
Before progressing further we need to consider carefully what archaeologists mean by the term 'continuity'. Studies of continuity have become rather fashionable in the last decade or so, and

5 *The plan of a Roman temple found during industrial development: Coleshill.*

6 *(Above right) Excavating a stone Roman coffin in a small mausoleum at Shepton Mallet.*

7 *(Below right) The head of the cult statue of Mercury from Uley. This was found among the foundations of a stone building, probably a church, above the remains of a Roman temple.*

often the existence of structures or groups of finds belonging to different time periods on a single site has led to the development of theories promoting continuous occupation in a preferred location. Unfortunately, more detailed consideration usually demonstrates that activity was not continuous at all. Thus at Poundbury, where there is evidence for settlement and burial from the Neolithic to the post-Roman periods, there were major desertions or the drastic relocation of structural elements in the Early Bronze Age, the Late Bronze Age, in the mid-Roman period and, probably, prior to the layout of the post-Roman settlement. In

comparison, at Uley there were major desertions or dislocations in the Bronze Age, the mid-fourth century AD and, probably, in the fifth century. What is most interesting about these long sequences, and others like them, is not the implication of continuity – a blanket term with little explanatory content – but the different and varied forms that recurrent use of a particular location may take.

Any one site may have been reused because it provided a readymade structure or earthwork that could be modified, or building materials that could be reworked in an efficient and economic fashion. This would denote an act of expediency. In the case of religious sites certain locations may have come to be regarded as sacred over a long time period and reuse by those of similar, or different, beliefs may reflect veneration. On the other hand, total destruction of a religious structure could reflect a deed of desecration, an act which may have been reinforced by the later erection of a new building dedicated to an alternative deity or cult. Furthermore, reused monuments, and especially those of the earthwork variety, may have been reused deliberately as the special container or 'sanctuary' for items of value. These items might include hoards of coins or religious paraphernalia such as silver plate or stone altars. It cannot be ruled out that, in some cases, reuse was due entirely to chance, but it does seem that, in general, sites and monuments that were perceived as being antique or primeval, and especially those possessing religious connotations in folk memory, were positively sought out for reuse of varying kinds. By these means the past could be brought into the present, and the new religious buildings and ideologies could be strengthened by powers of place and pedigree.

2

The placing of shrines

In medieval Europe every village was dominated architecturally by a Christian church and each city identified by the dramatic profile of the towers and steeples of its cathedral. In the Roman period temples would have fulfilled a similar ideological role, but their impact on the landscape would have been rather different. In Roman towns, temples would have been matched in scale and magnificence by other monumental buildings of secular function, while in the countryside only the larger settlements and small towns seem to have possessed their own shrines. Most rural temples were located in isolated, but geographically prominent, positions, such as on hilltops, next to major Roman roads or beside the more prosperous farmsteads. In comparison with the prevailing vernacular tradition of single-storey dwellings, usually constructed in timber, the massive tall temples with their red tile or grey stone roofs would have caught the eye from many miles around. This would not have been the case, however, in the pre-Roman period when the shrines and sacred places of the Iron Age Celts were hidden away among forests or in secret watery places, or placed within settlements where they would have looked little different from the houses and huts of the general populace.

Iron Age shrines

Classical authors such as Julius Caesar and Strabo described the sacred places of the Gauls that had been observed in the area of what is now southern France. These shrines were often located in woods or next to lakes and pools, or even on offshore islands. Sanctuary buildings and enclosures are also referred to, although not described in detail. The deposits of votive objects housed within the shrines or secreted in pools of water were of particular interest to the Roman writers, but they may not have noticed any small-scale timber-built shrines that possibly existed in the villages. It was the large isolated rural sanctuaries that seemed most unfamiliar, and therefore noteworthy, to the classical observers. In Britain, Dio Cassius referred to the existence of sanctuaries at the time of the revolt under Boudica, and to the offering of human sacrifices to the goddess of victory in a sacred wood, while the destruction of the sacred Druidic groves on the island of Anglesey by Suetonius Paulinus just before AD 61 was dramatized by Tacitus:

> The Druids were ranged in order, with hands uplifted, invoking the gods, and pouring forth horrible imprecations. The novelty of the sight struck the Romans with awe and terror...The Britons perished in the flames which they themselves had kindled. The island fell, and a garrison was established to retain it in subjection. The religious groves, dedicated to superstition and barbarous rites, were levelled to the ground.

Such total destruction was probably a rare occurrence, for, as will be shown below, the Romans attempted to absorb and adapt the religious beliefs and practices of the defeated tribes, rather than destroying them totally, and thus firing possible insurrection.

In Britain, there are only 17 sites where there is definite evidence of a shrine or a group of shrines that can be dated to the pre-Roman Iron Age period. The nature of these buildings and the votive finds associated with them will be discussed in the next chapter, while here we shall consider their siting in the landscape. The majority of the known shrines were located within centres of population; these were always large settlements and none have so far been identified within small rural farmsteads. The more impressive shrines, usually of square or rectangular plan, have been excavated within large hillforts which were important political centres in the Early and Middle pre-Roman

8 *Maiden Castle: the Iron Age, Roman and post-Roman structures excavated in the vicinity of the Roman temple.*

Iron Age. These include groups of shrines inside the hillforts at Danebury and South Cadbury, and the examples identified at Lancing (Sussex), Maiden Castle and outside the major Gloucestershire hillfort of Uley Bury. Such shrines were located in central positions within an area densely built up with Iron Age houses, storage pits and industrial or agricultural buildings, often ranged along a series of internal roads. This is well illustrated at Maiden Castle (8), where a sector of Iron Age 'townscape', with its associated circular shrine, was

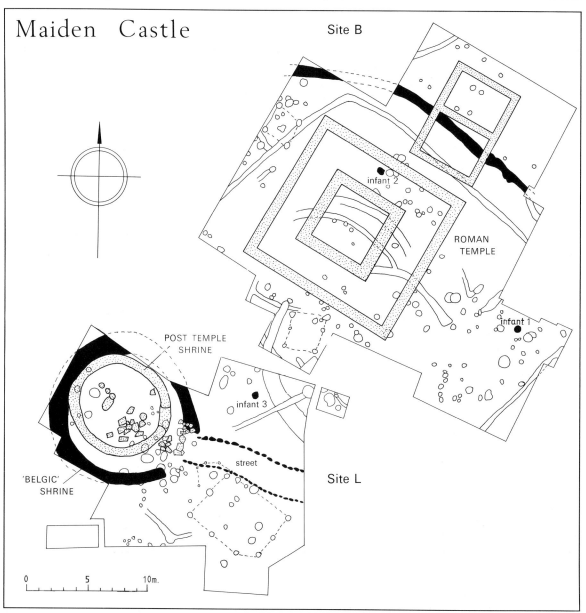

sealed beneath the remains of a later Roman temple and a post-Roman shrine.

In rural areas a few shrines are known from hilltop locations, Harlow being a notable example, but most of the others occur in settlements occupying more low-lying sites, often near to water courses and in areas which might well have been still forested in the Iron Age period.

At sites where occupation continued into the Roman period, the Iron Age shrines were invariably succeeded by a Romano-Celtic temple built in stone. This not only demonstrates the Roman policy of attempted eradication of Celtic practices by the wholesale adoption of their sacred places but also serves to highlight a potential problem. It may be that Iron Age shrines have so far only been recognized when they occur below a later temple and that religious buildings of a scale and type similar to surrounding domestic structures lie unrecognized on other Iron Age settlement sites. Nevertheless it seems clear that major groups of shrines were associated with political centres, such as at Danebury and South Cadbury, and that in a significant number of rural cases, shrines were located on or near to the boundaries between tribal areas.

Roman temples

For the Roman period a rather larger sample of shrines and temples is available and the locations of 86 well-documented examples are analysed in (**9**). It can be seen that the most frequently recorded locations are in the larger towns or on military sites such as forts. If the examples found in large unwalled settlements are included as well, these locations account for 41 per cent of the total. They include major classical temples in towns, as at Colchester; examples from many of the territorial *civitas* capitals such as Winchester, Silchester and Chichester; temples and shrines in or near Roman forts, especially along Hadrian's Wall at Carrawburgh and Housesteads; and further examples in the small towns and roadside settlements, for instance Chelmsford and Kelvedon in Essex, Springhead in Kent and Nettleton in Wiltshire. Fourteen examples (16 per cent) occurred in association with newly-founded structures in the countryside, either beside

9 *The location of Roman temples. The shaded zones denote the presence of Iron Age evidence.*

Roman roads (Titsey, Weycock Hill and Camerton) or in or adjacent to villa establishments, as at Chedworth, West Coker and Winterton. However, the remainder, a very significant 43 per cent, occurred in isolated rural locations, 21 per cent in apparent total isolation on hilltops or near springs and streams, and 22 per cent on or next to existing sites of prehistoric date. These sites included major Iron Age hillforts such as Maiden Castle and South Cadbury, but also many smaller and less politically significant sites such as Blaise Castle,

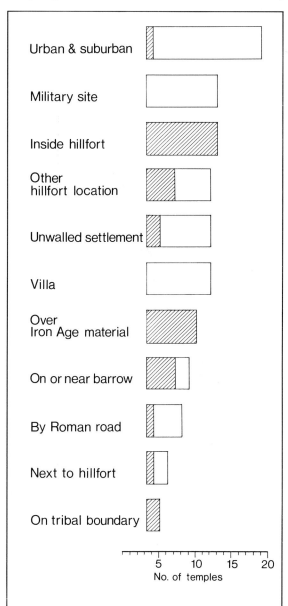

Lydney, Chanctonbury and Croft Ambrey. Also included in this rural category are temples which occurred immediately over or next to burial mounds of Neolithic or Bronze Age date, as at Brean Down, Mutlow Hill, and, again, Maiden Castle.

This overall pattern of location contrasts with that traced for the Iron Age period in that a third of the known Roman temple sites are found in isolated positions away from any settlement, whilst all the known Iron Age examples were associated with occupation sites. Although some isolated Iron Age examples may have existed in circumstances not conducive to discovery by archaeological techniques, the trend towards isolated shrine locations does seem to be a real characteristic of the Roman period. This trend is further confirmed by studying the variation in locations through time, which shows that urban temples declined in the later Roman period and that there was a contemporary growth of temple construction in the countryside. This growth coincided with a major peak of villa construction in the mid-fourth century AD and the growing numbers of both types of building, and their increased embellishment, may be closely linked. Such a link would act to illustrate and display the ties between religion and the political power of the landed aristocracy that developed during the Roman period.

It has been observed that, as in the Iron Age period, a significant number of the isolated rural temples were situated on or near to the boundaries between adjacent tribal or *civitas* areas. This could suggest that some temple sites functioned within the economy and society in general as regulators in the spheres of trade, social contact and the administration of justice. This would reflect the known multiple functions of Romano-Celtic temples in Gaul, where indeed many more occurred in boundary locations. At some temple sites in Britain, such as Gosbecks and Woodeaton, evidence of large-scale trading has been found, and the positioning of temples in the contact zones between tribal areas may have been related to a growth of peripheral markets, a phenomenon known to have taken place in this country as the Roman period progressed.

It is of particular interest to note that in a large number of cases, in fact 37 per cent of the total, Roman temples were erected directly over either buildings or other occupation evidence

of Iron Age date. Sometimes, as we have seen above, these Iron Age buildings functioned as shrines themselves. The incidence of the occurrence of Iron Age remains below Roman temples in different types of location is indicated in the chart (see **9**). In the case of rural temples, 57 per cent were on sites of former Iron Age occupation, although in some instances this appears to have been of a domestic rather than a religious nature. This high percentage is all the more remarkable when it is realized that in many past investigations of Roman temples, the excavators did not delve beneath the levels of the substantial wall footings and floors of the Roman structure. When considering Roman temples located in towns and forts, the incidence of Iron Age antecedents is far lower, only 9 per cent, but in these situations the lack of deep investigations below the levels of Roman masonry and floors is even more acute. It is only in the last decade that excavations in towns such as Silchester and St Albans have revealed the elusive traces of timber structures belonging to the earlier Roman periods, but large-scale investigations of any pre-Roman levels beneath the cities and *civitas* capitals are still unfortunately virtually unknown.

Two phases of pre-Roman occupation beneath the site of the basilica at Silchester appear to have been domestic or commercial in character, but in several other cases there are hints that the location of urban temples as well as other aspects of town planning were affected by the presence of influential pre-Roman shrines. At Silchester itself a pair of large Romano-Celtic temples was built next to the east gate, on the same site as the later medieval church of St Mary. However, the fact that these temples are not on the same alignment as the urban street plan, together with their peripheral location, suggest that they may lie on the site of a pre-existing sacred site. And at Bath (*Aquae Sulis*) the entire growth and development of the baths, temple complex and urban-style settlement can be attributed to the continuing exploitation of warm springs that were undoubtedly venerated in pre-Roman times. No structural remains of Iron Age date have yet been recovered, but the finding of 17 Celtic coins in the spring, and the association of the temple with the Celtic deity Sulis, together provide clues to the richness of the former sanctuary.

Continuity or reuse

The statistics discussed above strongly suggest that there was an element of continuity between the timber shrines of the Iron Age and the stone-built temples of the Roman era. It is often assumed that this was continuity of location combined with a continuity of religious function, but this assumption needs more detailed consideration. On a handful of sites excavation has indeed demonstrated that a Roman temple was erected directly over the remains of an Iron Age sanctuary, but in other cases the evidence for continuity rests on interpretation of the various ways in which the existing prehistoric monuments were reused. These classes of reuse include the location of temples inside hillforts; their situation adjacent to, but outside, hillforts; and reuse of the sites of former Bronze Age round barrows, or long barrows of Neolithic date. The reuse of Neolithic and Bronze Age monuments for religious purposes in the Iron Age or Roman periods has never been considered seriously, but this possibility will be raised below, following discussion of the other categories of 'assumed continuity'.

On some Roman temple sites, the finding of Iron Age coins or votive objects, and the recognition of a few post-holes or beam slots, has raised the possibility of the former existence of a Celtic shrine. This was the case at Harlow, where continuing excavation is now beginning to recover elements of the plan of underlying wooden structures, and also at Lydney where a handful of post-holes and a displaced door pivot-stone were recorded beneath the temple building. Recent excavations on two very different temple sites have provided more conclusive evidence for the overall plans of some impressive Iron Age sanctuaries below Roman temples. On Hayling Island an early Roman circular temple and its precinct have been very fully excavated and beneath its foundations lay one of the best examples so far investigated of an Iron Age temple (**10**; the Iron Age structure on the left; see also **21**). Constructed probably in the earlier part of the first century BC the central building resembled a domestic round-house. It was situated within a roughly square courtyard and in its centre lay a pit of unknown function. The courtyard and its outer boundary ditch contained a large and varied group of rich finds including items that can be associated with the trappings of an Iron Age warrior and his horse-drawn vehicle, together with jewellery and about 170 Celtic coins. Offerings of sheep and pig meat seem to have been common, as were pottery vessels that may have contained offerings of other foodstuffs or liquids. The temple survived until the Roman Conquest, after which it was rapidly replaced and transformed by the erection of a substantial stone temple, of a similar but larger circular plan, now occupying a large rectangular galleried temple enclosure or *temenos* (see **10**, right). The stone footings of the larger Roman temple lay exactly concentric with the rather smaller building of the Iron Age sanctuary. The whole site lies alone in an area of flat and fertile land. It is interesting to note that, if the votive finds had not been preserved and discovered by excavation, and if the massive Roman temple foundations had not lain above, then the Iron Age remains could well have been interpreted as a rural farmstead.

This proviso does not, however, apply in the case of the Iron Age ritual complex at Uley, where decidedly non-domestic structures occupied a ditched enclosure of unusual and non-functional proportions. Votive pits contained assemblages of objects including a few coins, pottery containers, unusual bone tools and iron weaponheads, and a series of human infant burials had been deposited as foundation offerings in the buildings. The posts of a focal timber structure were supported within a simple arrangement of separate post-holes forming a square (**11** and see below p. 31). There was no surviving evidence to indicate whether the posts had supported a roofed building or formed the fence of an open enclosure. Centrally within the square lay a pit which might have held a standing stone, timber post or living tree; if so the structure would probably have been open rather than roofed. In the early Roman period a rectangular Romano-Celtic stone temple was built directly above the site of the Iron Age shrine, and in exact alignment with it. Indeed, so exact was the superimposition that many of the post-holes belonging to the timber shrine must remain unexcavated beneath the mortared foundations of the Roman temple, which were not removed during the excavation (see **11**). Instances such as this help to explain the difficulties encountered in the past in attempting to define the plans of timber structures beneath the substantial stone remains of Romano-Celtic temples. It is only when the superimposition was not exact, as in the case of Brigstock, where the polygonal Roman shrine only partly obliterated an Iron Age oval enclosure, or where the two buildings were notably different in size, as at Hayling Island, that more complete ground-plans can be reconstructed.

Shrines and hillforts

One of the most frequent locations for Roman temples is inside the defences of an existing Iron Age hillfort. In many cases the evidence is slight, as at Blaise Castle (Henbury, Bristol); Croft Ambrey (Hereford and Worcs.) or at Bow Hill and Chanctonbury Ring in Sussex, and in others is merely circumstantial. For instance, at South Cadbury there is no direct evidence of a temple but the finding of late Roman coins and pottery on the hilltop over many centuries, indicates that there was activity on the site; the most likely explanation for these finds is that they were offerings made at a pagan shrine. During the excavations the post-Roman phases of the rampart were found to contain building debris that must have derived from a sophisticated Roman building, and the finds included a gilt-bronze letter 'A', of the type known to have been used to compose inscriptions on some other temple sites.

At Maiden Castle the Romano-Celtic temple was fully excavated (see 8) and its location within the massive hillfort is shown in 12. The late Roman buildings were set in the eastern half of the Iron Age hillfort, just north of the

10 *Plans of the Iron Age circular shrine and Roman temple on Hayling Island. The larger Roman building (right) lay directly over the Iron Age shrine (left).*

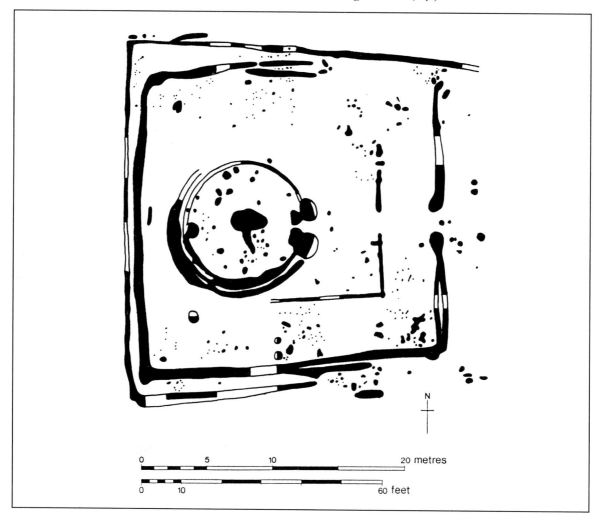

circular Late Iron Age shrine and the eastern end of the Neolithic bank barrow. The defences in the eastern sector were refurbished during the late Roman period and appear to have functioned as a *temenos* enclosure for the temple. The sanctuary was approached by a track from the eastern gateway of the hillfort, which was also renewed and remodelled at this time. At Lydney, the Roman temple also lay within a hillfort but in this case the prehistoric earthwork was a small promontory fort and the totally excavated temple complex, with its huge guesthouse and suite of baths, filled half of the area of the former defensive work (**13**). The Roman precinct wall and entrance seen in the drawing were, as at Maiden Castle, an adaptation of a main hillfort entrance and the associated defences. The heightening of the main defences across the promontory to the north, however, was accomplished during the post-Roman period. Although situated in an isolated valley system, the temple site at Lydney commanded a magnificent view across the Severn, and when the temple towers were in place it seems likely that the top of the Uley temple on the scarp of the Cotswolds might

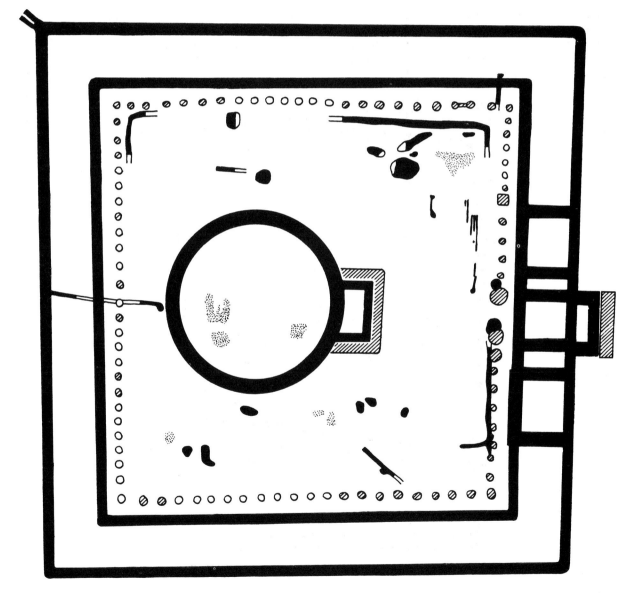

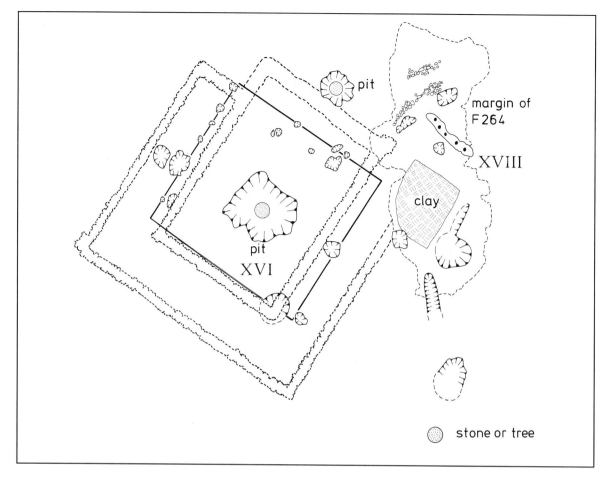

11 *The Iron Age structure and pits beneath the Roman temple at Uley. The outline of the Iron Age enclosure is indicated by a solid line, the edges of the temple foundations by broken lines.*

have been visible. Some of the Roman temples in Somerset were undoubtedly intervisible also, and this factor may have been a further influence on the precise siting of such sanctuaries.

In addition to those temples situated in the interiors of former Iron Age hillforts there is a further group that were sited adjacent to hillforts, but outside the main defences. At Uley, the Roman temple complex was placed about 500 m (1640 ft) north-east of the margins of one of the larger hillforts on the Cotswold scarp of Gloucestershire (**14**). The hillfort interior has never been excavated but has produced a fine collection of Neolithic flint- and stone-work, and later material including a series of

Celtic coins of Late Iron Age date. Aerial photographs have provided evidence of a complex palimpsest of compounds, ditches and circular structures indicative of intensive settlement. These appear to be mainly of prehistoric type, but some may represent structures of Roman, or even post-Roman, date. Little Roman material has been recovered, however, from the ploughed interior, and in the Roman period settlement was concentrated around the temple complex which, as we have seen, overlay an important prehistoric sanctuary. The extent of the Roman settlement is known only from surface finds and it may be that there was a substantial Late Iron Age settlement in this location, a massive suburb to the hillfort itself. Certainly the geophysical survey carried out around the temple area led to the discovery of anomalies that were more reminiscent of Iron Age timber buildings than of Roman structures built in stone.

Further south, in the county of Avon, another

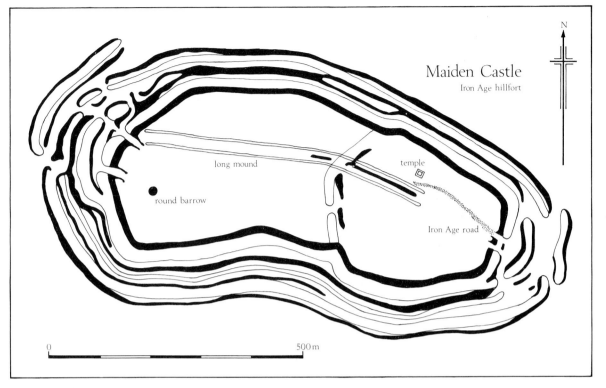

12 *Maiden Castle: barrows, hillfort and temple.*

13 *Reconstruction of the temple precinct at Lydney.*

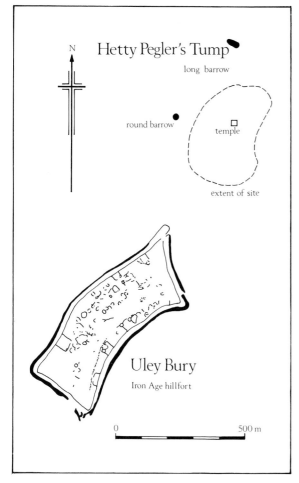

14 *Uley: barrows, hillfort and temple.*

recently excavated temple also lay adjacent to a major hillfort. The temple and *temenos* in Henley Wood was situated 140 m (460 ft) north of the eastern sector of the hillfort known as Cadbury, Congresbury (not to be confused with South Cadbury, Somerset), on the scarp of a limestone plateau (**15**). From the temple at least one other hillfort as well as the Somerset Levels and the South Wales coast would have been clearly visible. There was no evidence for settlement of Iron Age or Roman date around the temple site and no proven evidence of a pre-existing Celtic shrine. Reuse of the site, mainly for funerary purposes, is, however, well attested for the post-Roman period. Excavations inside the hillfort have demonstrated that it originated in prehistoric times but that it had been reused, with additional earthworks, in the late Roman and post-Roman periods. This occu-

pation was of high status and the structures examined probably included a shrine and other religious features. The interior of the hillfort is unploughed but contains earthwork remains of quarry pits, small mounds, hut circles and substantial rectilinear structures. The hut circles mainly occur in the western sector and are probably of Iron Age date, while the excavated late Roman to post-Roman structures lie in the area north of a central tree clump. Some of the Roman building material found amongst these late structures may have derived from the demolished temple at Henley Wood, and it is likely that the two sites were closely linked over a long period of time.

Shrines and barrows

Another aspect of temple location that has never been fully discussed is the occurrence of Roman religious buildings over, or adjacent to, the sites of prehistoric barrows. At Mutlow Hill (Cambs.) a circular temple was located next to a barrow and a series of Bronze Age cremation burials, contained in urns. Beneath the Iron Age and Roman shrines at Harlow were five Bronze Age pits, three of which contained urn fragments. An assemblage of Neolithic to Early Bronze Age flints was also found and these may have derived from an old ground surface sealed beneath a destroyed barrow which might have contained Bronze Age urned burials. It can be suggested further that a large pit dated to the Early Iron Age by the excavators would have been situated at the centre of such a barrow, and thus could represent robbing or reuse of the barrow centre in that period. At Haddenham (Cambs.) a series of timber-built Roman shrines was constructed over the ditch of a large Bronze Age barrow. An octagonal shrine constructed in the second century AD was later abandoned due to flooding and replaced in the late Roman period by two rectangular post-built shrines on the crown of the former barrow. On Slonk Hill (Sussex) the eastern of a pair of Bronze Age round barrows was surrounded by an Iron Age square post-built structure, similar to that excavated at Uley, and the whole area was enclosed by a fence. In the Roman period this fence line was redefined by a ditch, and a series of late Roman finds, including jewellery and a fragment of a votive leaf or feather, suggest that the site was still being venerated in that period.

The Roman temple and preceding Iron Age

ritual complex at Uley were sited close to the well-preserved Neolithic long barrow known as Hetty Pegler's Tump, and an almost levelled round barrow lies in the adjacent field (see **14**). Part of the Iron Age ritual enclosure reused an earlier U-shaped ditch which, on the basis of a limited distribution of flints, might have originated in the Neolithic period. Within this enclosure were several deep holes that may have contained standing stones or tree trunks, either dead or living. These enigmatic remains may relate to a sacred woodland enclosure or could possibly be the remnants of the ditch of a further Neolithic long barrow. On Brean Down the late Roman temple was sited immedi-

ately north of an unexcavated round barrow, the most easterly of a row of three along the brow of the peninsula (**16**). The temple also lay between a small Iron Age promontory fort and an Iron Age or Roman 'Celtic field' system that is preserved along the summit of the headland. Sealed within the sand cliff below are a series of Bronze Age settlements, with which the round barrows may have been connected, and a post-Roman cemetery which probably belonged to the latest phases of activity on the Roman temple site. Finally in this discussion of temples sited in association with prehistoric barrows, it must not be forgotten that the Iron Age shrine and Roman temple at Maiden Castle were located over and immediately north of the focal eastern end of one of the longest Neolithic barrows in Britain.

15 *Henley Wood: hillfort, temple and post-Roman shrine.*

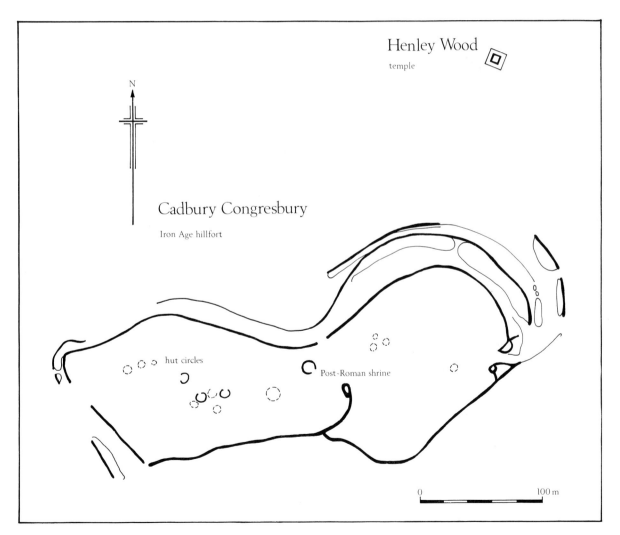

Whilst in some of the cases described above it might be argued that the juxtaposition of shrines and prehistoric barrows occurred by chance, the instances where religious timber and stone structures were built directly over the earlier monument, as at Harlow, Slonk Hill, Haddenham and Uley, indicate that a tradition of deliberate reuse was strong. The existence of such a tradition is also supported by the evidence of the use of Bronze Age round barrows for secondary Roman burials. These occur regularly but sporadically in all areas. In the south well-authenticated cases include 3 in Wiltshire, 5 from Gloucestershire, 5 in Somerset and 12 in Dorset. Roman finds from the upper levels of excavated long barrows suggest that these Neolithic monuments, and particularly those possessing stone chambers, were the subject of activity in the Roman period. At West Kennet (Wilts.) Roman coins in the façade area of the tomb suggested more than casual loss, and at Wayland's Smithy (Oxon.) a ditch dug across the front of the megalithic façade in the Roman period was subsequently filled with sarsen boulders and fragments of human bone. In Gloucestershire, no fewer than eight long barrows have produced evidence for interference or reuse during the Roman period, including a secondary grave discovered at Hetty Pegler's Tump, next to the Uley Roman temple site. At Julieberrie's Grave, Chilham (Kent) early Roman burials in the barrow ditch were associated with a hearth and midden, and Roman sherds were also found amongst the stones of the Neolithic burial chamber. Some at least of these examples must demonstrate overt veneration of standing monuments surviving from the past. Other monuments were selected as suitable sites for the concealment of objects of a valuable or religious nature. Some barrows were used for the deposition of Roman coin hoards and in Gloucestershire two groups of carved Roman stone altars were found hidden within the mounds of Bronze Age barrows at Bisley Common and Tidenham Chase.

16 *Brean Down: Bronze Age settlement and barrows, hillfort, temple and post-Roman cemetery.*

Shrines and henges
Turning lastly to a consideration of the possible reuse and continuing sanctity of late Neolithic

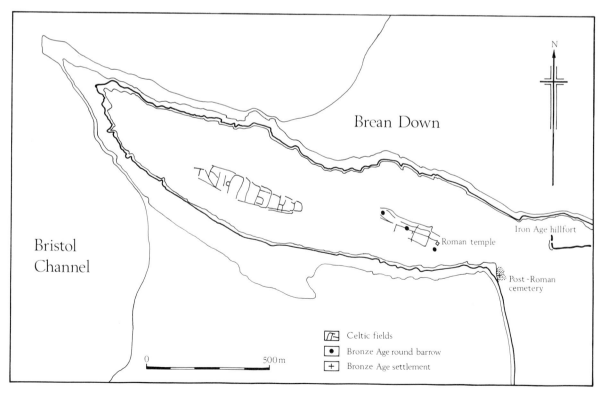

henge monuments, it is interesting to note that many of the larger monuments have produced material of Iron Age or Roman date. Some of this evidence is summarized in the table (**17**). At Durrington Walls and Mount Pleasant there was no evidence to suggest that the Iron Age structures found inside the monuments were of a religious nature and the excavator rightly concluded that they were domestic buildings. Similarly the Saxon grave inside Mount Pleasant was probably located there by chance, an outlier of an extensive cemetery that is situated further to the west.

At Llandegai the Iron Age buildings were sited within an extant earthwork bank which appears to have been reused as a readymade perimeter enclosure for an ordinary Iron Age farmstead. However, the slighting of the bank in the Roman period and use of the site for a post-Roman cemetery with an associated building might hint at some folk memory of the earthwork's former significance. The henge bank at Maumbury Rings survived into the Roman period and was modified for use in a purely secular way as an amphitheatre for the Roman town of Dorchester. At Thornborough the earthwork appears to have survived intact into the medieval period but no evidence for use in the Iron Age or Roman periods was recovered during excavation.

There are two sites where fairly minor cuttings across the ditches of henge monuments have produced substantial evidence for Roman activity. One of these is Condicote where the single narrow ditch cutting hit a major Roman pit which had impinged upon one edge of the henge ditch. The finds from this pit included significant quantities of Roman pottery and a Celtic coin. At Arminghall the earthwork survived into the Roman period and the ditch silting contained much material of this date. From one cutting alone came 23 tile fragments, 9 coins and 1029 potsherds, while the outer ditch was found to contain a Roman hearth. The nature of the Roman presence on these two sites cannot of course be determined, but the possibility of religious reuse should be borne in mind during any further investigations on these or similar sites.

The henge at Avebury survived intact until just after AD 1300 but no direct evidence for

17 *Post-Bronze-Age evidence from henge monuments.*

SITE	COUNTY	IRON AGE STRUC-TURE	IRON AGE POTTERY	ROMANO-BRITISH STRUC-TURE	ROMANO-BRITISH POTTERY	ROMAN OR POST-ROMAN BURIALS	MEDIEVAL POTTERY	DATE OF DESTRUCTION OR LEVELLING
Arminghall	Norfolk			X	X			post-Roman
Avebury	Wilts.				X		X	(earthwork extant); stones after AD 1300
Condicote	Glos.			X	X			post-Roman
Durrington Walls	Wilts.	X	X					(extant)
Llandegai	Gwyn-edd	X	X	X	X	X		probably Roman
Maumbury Rings	Dorset		X	X	X		X	(extant)
Mount Pleasant	Dorset	X	X	X	X	X		probably Iron Age or Roman
Stonehenge	Wilts.		X		X	X	X	began in Roman
Thornborough	Yorks.							Medieval

Iron Age or Roman use has been uncovered. Some Roman sherds were found in the excavated ditch silts, but none at all of Iron Age date. However, it was probably its pagan usage that led to the deliberate and systematic destruction instigated by ecclesiastical leaders during the fourteenth century. Even so, the careful burial of each stone intact implies that the destroyers still held respect for the components of the monument. Reuse for agriculture and domestic habitation followed, but the medieval church remained 'safely' located just outside the bounds of the monument. At Stonehenge there is much more direct evidence for use in the Iron Age and Roman periods. This is all the more remarkable in the light of the results of a major fieldwork project recently completed in the environs of Stonehenge – results which indicate a veritable absence of Iron Age and Roman activity in the zone around the monument. The evidence consists mainly of an assemblage of potsherds from the secondary fills of a set of Bronze Age holes that were dug to house a circle of bluestones that was never implemented, together with one male burial from just outside them. The excavator felt that destruction of the monument probably began in the Roman period, but the distribution of fallen and missing stones is remarkably uneven and may reflect a pattern of selective reuse: the tidying up of a partly ruined structure to function actively as a sanctuary in the Roman period. Certainly more Roman pottery has been found at Stonehenge than medieval items.

The henge site at Knowlton in Dorset survives today as a fine upstanding earthwork and was used as the site for the medieval parish church (**colour plate 1**). This isolated church, ruined since the eighteenth century, has always been located away from the settlement it served, which now survives only as earthworks along the River Allen 430 m (1410 ft) north-west of the church. Church Henge at Knowlton has never been excavated so we do not know whether there is evidence for usage during the Iron Age or Roman periods. If there was, then the church may have developed from a converted Roman shrine. Alternatively, even if no Roman structures were present, then the placing of the medieval church might suggest that Christian placation of continuing pagan rituals was intended.

3

The structure of shrines

Iron Age shrines

Few attempts have ever been made to draw a reconstruction of an Iron Age shrine, the simple reason for this being that it is not known how the superstructure was organized, or how the shrines looked. Of the 17 known examples where a ground-plan can be reasonably reconstructed, 13 were of square or rectangular plan and 4 were circular. Two of the circular type, located at Hayling Island and inside Maiden Castle, have already been illustrated in the previous chapter and the difficulty of separating such circular religious buildings from the generality of Iron Age round-houses has been emphasized. The last 20 years of excavation has revolutionized our knowledge of the four-sided structures and some of the examples will be described below. Shrines of Iron Age date located within settlements usually occurred in open areas set aside for ceremonial use and were spatially separated from domestic buildings. Analysis of building sizes has shown that they tended to be small and probably were not intended to hold large congregations of worshippers. Alignment of the four-sided buildings was variable but there was an overwhelming tendency for entrances to face eastwards.

Two timber structures excavated within the Late Iron Age enclosures at Uley were of unusual square and trapezoidal plan (18). Post-holes belonging to the central structure (XVI) were found to contain iron projectile heads and a complete pot, while both buildings were associated with the remains of human infants that may have been deposited at the time of construction. From the square structure XVI the bones of a seven- to nine-month-old baby were recovered, while the bodies of two slightly older infants had been buried under posts of structure XVII to the north. Other human remains from the site included fragments from the skeleton of a nine-month-old baby found in the enclosure ditch, and a shaft of a femur and one adult molar from a votive pit.

The square timber structure XVI comprised a simple arrangement of separate post-holes forming a square. As mentioned above there is no evidence to indicate whether the posts supported a roofed building or formed the fence of an open enclosure. In the centre of the square lay a pit which may have contained a standing stone, timber post or living tree and the structure may therefore have been open; it certainly appears to have been constructed around the focal feature. Further north, and constructed slightly later, structure XVII contained no finds apart from the infant burials. In contrast to the post construction of the square structure, this building was supported by closely-spaced circular posts held in continuous bedding trenches.

The trapezoidal building structure XVII cannot be paralleled easily, although its trench construction can be matched in ritual buildings at Danebury and South Cadbury (see 18). The square building structure XVI was of similar size to shrines at Heathrow (Middlesex) and Danebury (RS1). Whilst the building at Heathrow could have been of two phases or have functioned as a small trench-built shrine within a post-built fenced enclosure, at Danebury structure RS1 appears to have been free-standing. The interior is relatively undisturbed by pits and there were no traces of any interior substructure. However, at Uley the interior of the square enclosure defined by posts was heavily disturbed by Roman and post-Roman features and the possibility of the former existence of a subsidiary structure around the focal

IRON AGE SHRINES

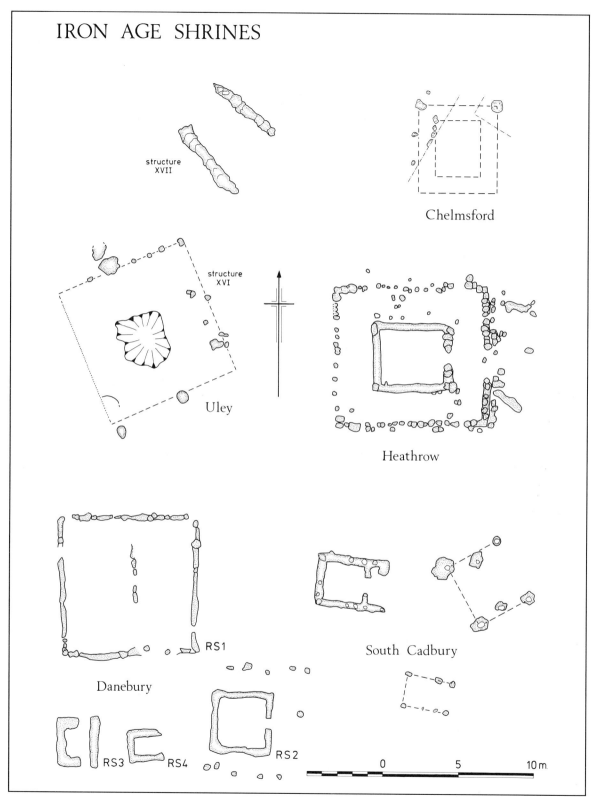

structure
XVII

Chelmsford

structure
XVI

Uley

Heathrow

RS1

Danebury

South Cadbury

RS3   RS4   RS2

0   5   10 m

pit cannot be ruled out. Although the Uley shrine was of similar dimensions to RS1 at Danebury, all the rectangular shrines there were supported in bedding trenches, and some were possibly plank-built. At South Cadbury two of the rectangular shrines were built of posts and one was a bedding-trench structure; a further post-built structure, apparently possessing an internal enclosure, has been suggested at Chelmsford, Essex.

At Danebury, South Cadbury, Heathrow and Little Waltham, the shrines occupied central positions within major domestic or proto-urban settlements. In other cases religious buildings were situated near the centre of purpose-built ditched enclosures which on occasion reached massive proportions (**19**). At Hayling Island and Uley the ditches of such ritual enclosures have been investigated in detail by modern excavation. At Uley a complex sequence of growth and modification was shown to have taken place: by the Late Iron Age the open-ended oval ditch that may have originated in the Neolithic period had silted up but must have been visible still as hollows. The lines of the ditch were reused for the cutting of slots for substantial timber palisades that were probably erected in the first century BC. A little later the enclosure was extended and almost doubled in size by the addition of two square-cut ditches which contained a single palisade on the west and a double palisade to the north (see (**19**), upper left). On the eastern side, a separate and very much deeper segment of ditch contained deposits of votive material. In the northern part of the enclosure at least, the ditches were accompanied by an external bank. The enclosure appears to have been designed to surround the square timber shrine discussed previously and, during the use of that building, a pit for the deposition of votive offerings was cut into the inner edge of the deepest, eastern ditch segment. Later still, the trapezoidal shrine was constructed over part of the infilled northern ditch of the enclosure.

The Uley enclosure belongs to a recognized group of ritual centres which has been defined in Britain and on the European continent. The ditches beneath the Roman temple enclosures at Harlow and Colchester (Temple 6) were both curvilinear, although substantially disparate

18 *Plans of square and rectangular shrines of Iron Age date.*

in size (see **19**). More details of construction have been obtained from Lancing (Sussex) and Hayling Island: at Lancing there was evidence for palisade posts and at Hayling Island the excavators have suggested that the enclosure limit was defined by a hedge supplemented by timber fencing. A fence was also postulated at Slonk Hill (Sussex). The best parallels for the sub-rectangular enclosure at Uley are provided by the long ditched enclosures of continental Europe. These are well exemplified by the tenth-century BC enclosures of Aulnay-aux-Planches, France, with a ditch which may have contained a palisade, and terminal stone monoliths; and the Czechoslovakian site of Libenice where an area of intersecting pits formed a sunken sanctuary within which libations were poured (see **19**). This sanctuary contained a standing stone as well as two holes intended to support posts which were probably carved to represent deities, and were adorned with the two bronze neck-rings that were discovered nearby.

Classical Roman temples

The term temple invokes a vision of the great classical edifices of the Mediterranean world – buildings like those surviving on Sicily or at Paestum, in Italy, or the imposing buildings surmounting the Acropolis in Athens. However, in the far distant province of Britain there is only one well-known example of a temple that would have resembled these. This was the massive temple dedicated to the deified emperor Claudius, erected in the early years after the establishment of Roman Colchester. The only surviving remnant of this building is a very substantial *podium*, or platform, measuring 33 m by 24 m (108 ft by 79 ft), which was incorporated in the foundations of the Norman castle keep (now the Castle Museum). The stone *podium* contained four 'vaults', actually voids probably filled with sand, which could have supported a vast structure with a rectangular *cella* at the rear, flanked by rows of columns and with a roofed open-sided area in front approached by a flight of steps. This would have led to a pedimented façade supported on eight towering Corinthian columns. The cult of the emperor and also, probably, the foreign ostentation of the classical architecture itself, did not appeal to the native population, and the erection of this wholly Roman edifice may well have fired the Boudican revolt (AD 61), an

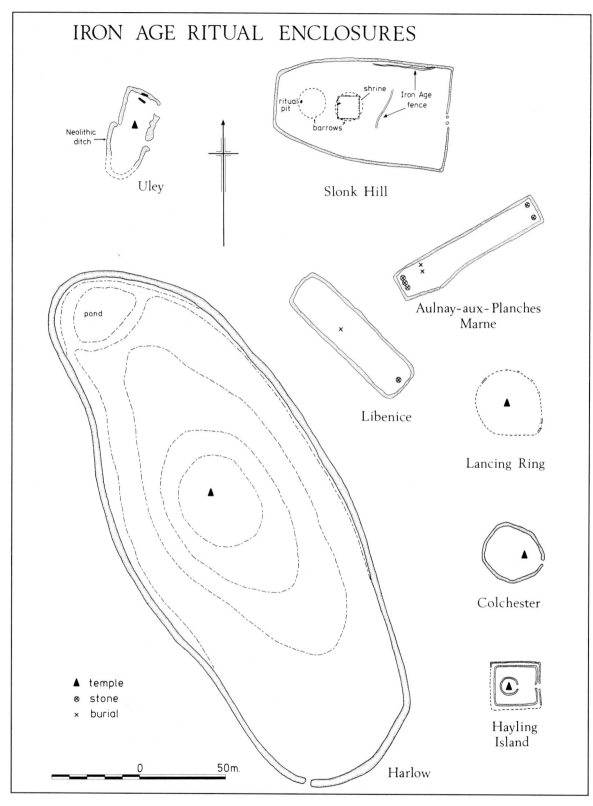

IRON AGE RITUAL ENCLOSURES

19 *(Left) Iron Age ritual enclosures.*

20 *Aerial photograph showing cropmark of the Roman temple on Hayling Island.*

21 *Hayling Island: artist's reconstruction of the Iron Age shrine.*

uprising which led to the destruction of many towns in the south and east of Britain during the early years of the Roman occupation.

Another important temple built before AD 60 was that recently investigated at Hayling Island, following its discovery by aerial photography (**20**). This building was constructed on a truly massive scale and comprised a circular stone *cella* 13.9 m (46 ft) in diameter enclosed within a square courtyard (**21** and **22**). The *cella* had walls made of local limestone covered with red plaster on the outside, and a multi-coloured plaster interior; there was no *podium* or ambulatory. The courtyard wall supported five rooms on the eastern entrance side. One of these would have functioned as an entrance hall, possibly with internal columns, and the others could have fulfilled administrative purposes.

There are no parallels for such a large-scale circular temple as this elsewhere in Britain, and the closest comparable examples are situated in western and central France. Best known of

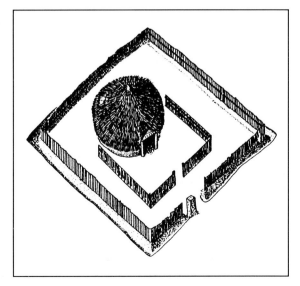

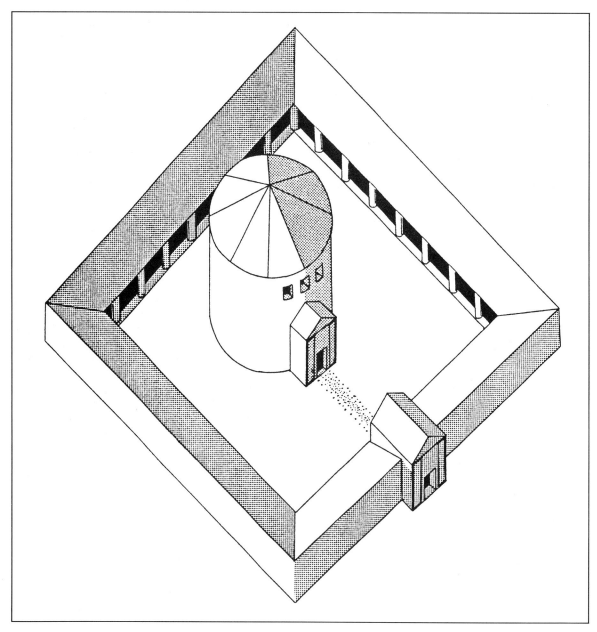

22 *Hayling Island: artist's reconstruction of the early Roman temple.*

these is the surviving tower *cella* at Perigueux, although that temple did also possess an ambulatory. The presence of such a continental-looking temple on the south coast may have been linked to the construction of the first-century palace at nearby Fishbourne, home probably of the client king Cogidubnus. The workmen on both buildings were probably Gaulish and the cult practised at Hayling Island may have been a Celtic version of a Roman dedication to Mars, as is evidenced for some of the great circular temples of western and central France.

Very few other religious buildings of pure classical style can be identified but these include the remarkable group constructed at Bath (**23**). Here reconstruction of the presumed Iron Age healing complex, which had been damaged by the alignment of an early Roman road, may have been the result of official involvement following the Boudican revolt. Although the temples erected here were in an astonishingly elaborate and flagrantly classical style, the buildings were on a smaller scale and less regular than the great courtyard surrounding the temple of Claudius at Colchester. The main temple, dedicated to Sulis Minerva, was a small four-columned temple in Corinthian style set on a high *podium* near to the centre of a colonnaded precinct measuring 52 m by 70 m (171 ft by 230 ft). In front of it was a paved area with the main altar which was used for sacrifices, while in the south-east corner of the precinct the hot springs were tamed by the construction of a lead-lined reservoir 2 m (6½ ft) deep.

The temple steps led up to a porch fronted by four great columns which drew the eye upwards to the great Gorgon's head on the pediment. Within the *cella* would have stood a statue of the goddess Sulis Minerva, and the gilded bronze head found in an eighteenth-century sewer trench nearby probably belonged to this cult figure. To the south lay the Roman baths which were linked, both ideologically and architecturally, to the great healing cult centred on the temple and the spring. In the early second century AD a second precinct was laid out to the east. This is now masked by the west end of the medieval abbey, but appears to have contained a circular temple, or *tholos*, embellished with rich sculptural ornament and without parallel in Britain.

About AD 300 the temple to Sulis Minerva was enclosed by a kind of ambulatory, and a new façade with steps leading up between two flanking rooms now aggrandized the main front. The spring was covered by a massive vaulted hall and this would have restricted access to the sacred pool, which became a more secret and mysterious place – shady, dripping and resounding with subtle echoes. After about a hundred years, the reservoir hall structure began to decay and to support the walls a massive new northern façade incorporating three strong buttresses was erected. This was balanced by a second façade on the other side of the precinct. The visual effect from the eastern precinct entrance would have been a funnelling of the sight-lines forwards and upwards to the imposing pediment of the central temple. The architectural complexity and brilliance displayed at Bath was exceptional, but no doubt influenced the style of many of the native temples and shrines that abounded both in the towns and countryside.

Romano-Celtic temples

Many smaller temples were built in the so-called Romano-Celtic style, typified by a series of buildings found throughout Gaul and Roman Germany. The defining characteristics of a Romano-Celtic temple are an internal *cella* with a concentric ambulatory. The most common form is rectangular, with the slightly greater dimension from façade to rear, while examples of circular and polygonal form occur less frequently, and mainly in western France and southern Britain (**25**). The circular and polygonal examples were usually situated in rural locations, whilst those in the larger towns were almost always rectangular. It is assumed that the ambulatory was intended to provide shelter for ritual processions and as a location for the attachment and display of votives, but that the *cella* would only have been entered by the religious specialists, and individuals wishing to approach the enshrined deity with offerings and supplication.

The reconstruction of Romano-Celtic temples is a very difficult task. This is due partly to the scant remains of wall footings and floor levels, and to the fact that in many cases excavation has been small-scale, but also a large proportion of the excavations were undertaken prior to the development of systematic recording methods for architectural and structural detail. Twenty-five years ago it was proposed that the ground-plans of such temples might have supported structures of one of three main alternatives (**24**). Type I involved a *cella* in the form of a high tower rising above the ambulatory roof, while Type II possessed a lower *cella* such that the whole structure could be covered by a single roof span. The third type was characterized by an open courtyard, presumed to contain a sacred pool of water, a standing monument or statue, or a living tree, surrounded by a covered ambulatory opening inwards. The results of more recent research and new excavations have served to render the Type II and Type III interpretations very unlikely, and it is now generally agreed that Romano-Celtic temples were dominated by high-rising central towers.

Controversy has also surrounded the question of whether the ambulatory was open to

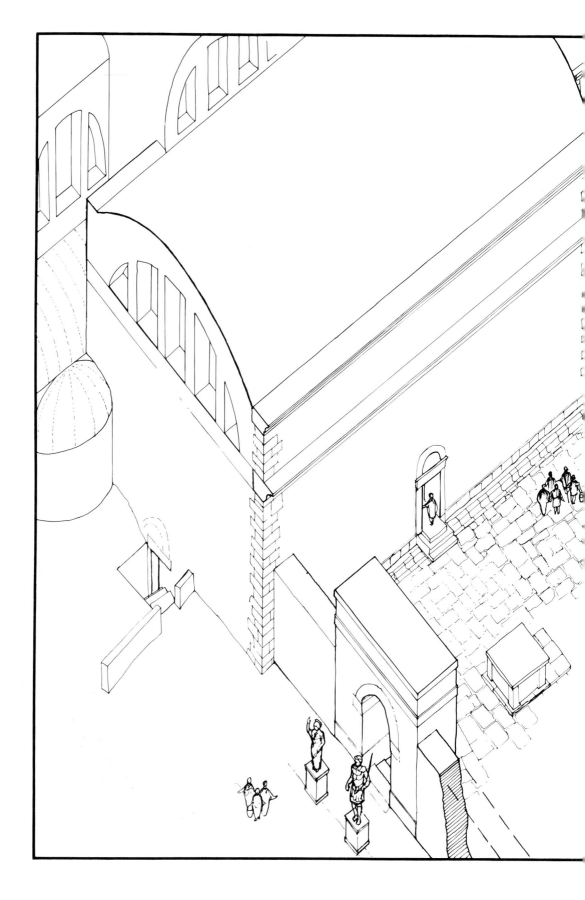

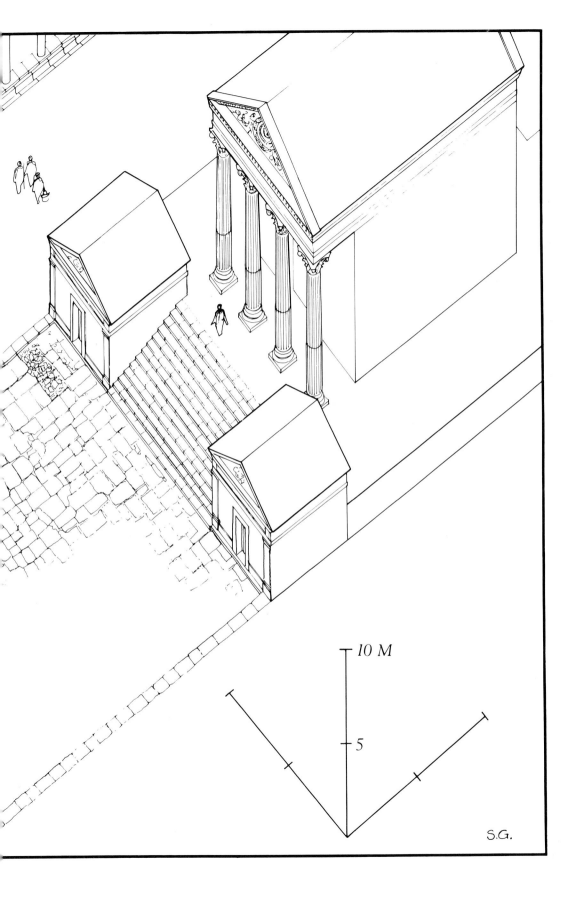

10 M

5

S.G.

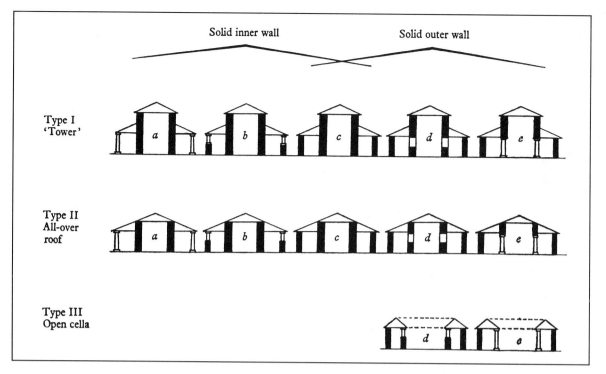

Solid inner wall   Solid outer wall

Type I
'Tower'

Type II
All-over
roof

Type III
Open cella

23 *(Previous page) Bath: axonometric reconstruction of the temple (period 2).*

24 *Hypothetical types of Romano-Celtic temple, defined by Lewis in 1966.*

the elements and defined by a colonnade or whether it was enclosed by a solid outer wall. Also, in either of these cases, the possible existence of major openings between ambulatory and cella, as proposed at Pagan's Hill, has also been the subject of discussion. Careful analysis of the available evidence has led to the conclusion that in Britain, and possibly in Gaul and Germany, most Romano-Celtic temples possessed ambulatories with solid outer walls. However, in a few cases, it can be proved that porticos did exist.

Other temple forms

Several recently excavated temples have proved to belong to a rather different type of plan, dominated by the absence of the ambulatory along the front elevation. A selection of these divergent plans is shown in **29** and the type will be discussed here with detailed reference to the building excavated at Uley.

Probably in the early second century AD the Iron Age timber shrine at Uley was replaced, on exactly the same alignment, by a square stone structure. The foundations were fragmentary, razed to ground level and much disturbed

by modifications executed in later periods, and by many centuries of arable agriculture but the plan could be resolved into two major building phases (see **29**). The first involved a nearly rectangular *cella* with an ambulatory of even width on three sides only. The main entrance was located on the north-east side and probably consisted of an applied doorcase, supported by posts as shown by two major post-holes, attached to a screen wall, all foundations of which had been destroyed except for two stone plinths. Reconstruction of the temple floor level suggests that two steps would have been necessary to allow access to the courtyard level in front of the temple. No original floor levels survived and the only internal features that could have related to the temple as it was initially conceived were the central pit, which may have contained a lead tank or other water container, and a mortar base centrally positioned in the south-western ambulatory. This base may have been the remnant of a foundation for a plinth intended for the display of the major cult statue. In a later phase the temple was extended and aggrandized by the addition of a rectangular projecting foundation which

25 *Artist's reconstruction of the interior of the octagonal temple of Apollo at Nettleton Scrubb.*

26 *Drawing of a relief from Titelberg, Germany, showing a Romano-Celtic temple.*

could have supported an open portico raised well above the level of the main courtyard and approached by a flight of four steps. The primary screen wall was remodelled probably at this time, but no definite traces of foundation had survived.

At first it was suggested that the extremely unusual temple plan might best be explained in terms of a roofed and totally enclosed ambulatory surrounding an open courtyard dominated by a focal tree, post or menhir surviving from the prehistoric phases. Such a reconstruction would have related to the Class III temple plans mentioned above (see **24**). However, detailed analysis has shown that the levels and other information upon which the case for a courtyard interpretation had been related not to the period of construction and use of the stone temple but to later modifications. A relief from Titelberg in Germany (26) shows a temple with a tall central *cella*, but no front ambulatory, which thus may be equated with the primary phase at Uley. The side ambulatories are shown to be gabled, rather than having the pent roof more commonly associated with temple ambulatories, and drainage would have been achieved by means of a valley gutter between the inner slope of the ambulatory roof and the upper *cella* wall. This gutter could have disgorged at the front into two tanks and by this means the sacred water falling on the roofs above the venerated cult image could have been conserved and perhaps used as a source for the filling of tanks or pools associated with the temple ritual. The Titelberg relief also appears to show a temple embellished by a classical doorcase and, overall, the resemblance between this depiction and one possible reconstruction of the temple at Uley is very striking.

A reconstruction drawing shows one temple phase with associated contemporary buildings (27); the walls would have been of roughly-squared oolitic limestone and the roof built with a timber structure and polygonal red sandstone tiles. The exterior wall surfaces may have been coated with pale-coloured plaster, or stucco, from the beginning and would certainly have been so treated in the later, more classical, phases. By then, the elevations may have been embellished also by moulded pilasters rising from a plinth, although the only surviving evidence for pilasters was a projection from the foundations at the south-west corner of the building. The roofs of the ambulatories, doorcase and portico are shown to be gabled, as in the Titelberg relief. The *cella* is reconstructed as surmounted by a regular pyramidal roof and the ends of the ambulatory roofs are hipped, but an alternative reconstruction (28) shows a more classical scheme whereby the *cella* is provided with a gabled elevation from conception and this is matched by gables at the front ends of each ambulatory. All these gables could have been embellished with classical ornament. Temples of this kind would have possessed rather lower towers, so that the slopes of the

27 *Artist's reconstruction of the temple and courtyard buildings at Uley (phase 5d–e).*

cella roof would be more or less in line with the outer slopes of the ambulatory roof. In the simpler reconstruction drawing (see **27**) there are rows of small square or round-headed windows set high in both *cella* and ambulatory. The more classical building with its elegant pilastered elevations would more probably have been windowless, with the exception of a row of small openings in the upper *cella* wall which would have been largely hidden from view by the ambulatory roof. In all cases the valley gutter, which was probably stone, debouched into cisterns located at either side of the temple steps. These cisterns have been depicted in stone, but might equally have been made of lead. In drawing the portico the proportions

28 *An alternative reconstruction of the Uley temple, incorporating classical features.*

were influenced by the axonometric reconstructions of the temple of Sulis Minerva at Bath (see **23**) and it may be that the original portico was constructed by individuals who were familiar with that building.

Parallels for the unusual temple plan deduced at Uley may be found most readily amongst a group of temples that show evidence for porches and antechambers. These arrangements would have allowed direct access, or a direct view, into the central *cella*, but not into the rear and side ambulatories, which appear to have been reserved either for the priests or for the secure storage of votive offerings. A selection of such plans, shown at the same scale as plans of the two major phases at Uley, is provided in **29**. In the Altbachtal at Trier, Germany, the plan of temple 2 shows a portico with direct access to the *cella* and restricted doorways leading to

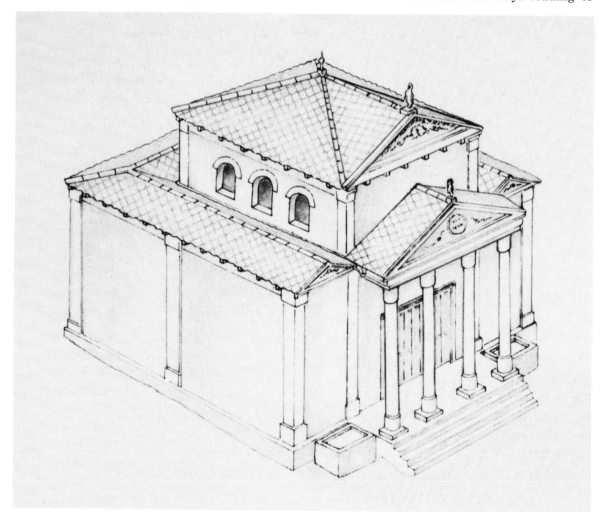

ROMAN TEMPLES

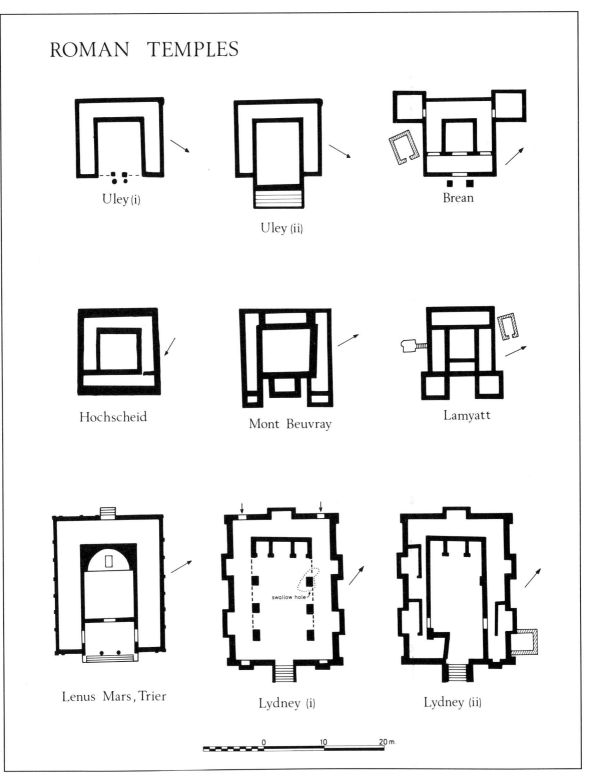

29 *Plans of selected Roman temples in Britain, France and Germany.*

the enclosed ambulatories, and a very similar pattern is displayed at Caerwent. Also in continental Europe, three-sided ambulatories are known at Mont Beuvray (see **29**), and Trier temple H, and Eu. A similar arrangement of the ambulatory space is seen at Brean Down and Lamyatt Beacon, both in Somerset, although in the case of Brean, the forechamber extends right across the front of the building. In this respect further continental parallels may be invoked, including the plan of the temple at Hochscheid (all on **29**). Finally it is illuminating to consider the disposition of space within the great temple at Nodens at Lydney. Here the original temple plan (**29**, Lydney (1)) would have supported a unique semi-classical building with large openings between the ambulatory and the *cella*. However, following an almost immediate collapse as one of the major piers fell into the earlier iron mine below, the temple was rebuilt with an enclosed *cella* (Lydney (II)). Further, the ambulatories were cut off from the entrance area by new partition walls so that the worshippers would have obtained a direct, but limited, view of the triple sanctuary occupying the far end of the *cella*. Yet again, as at Uley, the ambulatories seem to have been designed for secret priestly activities and not for public access.

Internal features and structures have only rarely been recorded during the excavation of temples in Britain, but those investigated in continental Europe have sometimes produced more useful evidence. Centrally placed pits or wells are known from eight temples in France and Germany. At Alesia in France a central pit predated one of the temples, but continued in use as has also been suggested at Uley. At Hochscheid (see **29**) the centre of the *cella* was occupied by a basin into which a spring rose, and at Montbuoy a centrally located *piscina* was fed from a spring in a nearby enclosure. The positions of cult images or altars have not been deduced for many temples in this country, while in Europe foundations for plinths or bases are widespread. Of 25 examples of such statue or altar bases, 11 were centrally located in the cella while the others occupied the margin of the cella, most often on the western side. Thus the postulated positioning of the Uley cult image within the ambulatory remains anomalous and uncertain. Although there are records of the finding of statues themselves in ambulatory locations, these may not have been

in primary contexts. At Avallon a whole series of figures, life-size or larger, were found within the ambulatories, and at Bierbacher Klosterwald the torso of a statue of Mercury was found outside the northern wall of the *cella*. Whether this statue had been housed there previously or had stood upon a base found just inside the *cella* cannot be determined. The scant evidence for furniture and fittings employed within Romano-Celtic temple interiors will be considered further in the next chapter.

Whilst the British Romano-Celtic temples of concentric plan seem to be a standard type of religious building, closely related to examples in Gaul and Germany, there are also numerous examples of more simple shrines which seem to have continued the building traditions of the native population. These shrines were similar in plan to the Iron Age types, that is either a simple circular or rectangular building, but were often now executed in stone, and sometimes evidence for sophisticated flooring has also survived. A few examples are known to have been timber-framed and occasionally slight evidence for a flimsy attempt at an ambulatory has also been recovered. Shrines of this simple type were particularly concentrated in the East Midlands, in the territory of the Coritani, and it is here also that most of the simple polygonal shrines occurred; for instance, clear examples have been excavated at Brigstock and Collyweston (Northants.). Although irregular polygonal houses of timber construction are known from Iron Age Britain, it is more likely that the regular polygonal plans of some of the shrines were related to the polygonal Romano-Celtic temples of western Gaul and southern Britain.

The size of temples

An analysis of the dimensions and floor areas of shrines and temples of Iron Age and Roman date has proved of some interest. The classical and sub-classical Romano-Celtic temples of Roman Britain range in size from 25 sq. m (269 sq. ft) to a massive 790 sq. m (8504 sq. ft) for the Temple of Claudius at Colchester. From 40 examples that have been measured, three main concentrations of size can be identified: at 50 sq. m (538 sq. ft); between 100 and 175 sq. m (1076 and 1884 sq. ft); and between 250 and 300 sq. m (2691 and 3229 sq. ft). Temples of square, circular and polygonal plan all occur in each different size range. However, the simple temples of non-classical type form a much smaller group and were characterized by more limited floor areas. These cluster around 100 sq. m (1076 sq. ft) (seven examples) with five more possessing floor areas of less than 25 sq. m (269 sq. ft). The shrines of Iron Age date, however, were even smaller, with only two examples having areas just above 100 sq. m (1076 sq. ft) (Heathrow and Thistleton), and most had floors measuring less than 50 sq. m. (538 sq. ft). Thus in the Roman period the areas covered by roofed shrine buildings increased. This would have allowed more room for priests and other specialists to carry out their ritual activities and also some space for members of the public to enter prescribed sectors of the buildings. Even so, entire congregations could seldom have been accommodated and major festivals and ceremonies would have been celebrated in the open areas of the temple precincts. An interesting result of the analysis is the apparent contrast between stone-built Romano-Celtic temples and non-classical shrines of Roman date. The latter may have been suited for the more limited, and probably more secretive, rituals of the type enacted in the preceding Iron Age periods, while the Romano-Celtic temples would have provided facilities for more Romanized acts of veneration and worship.

Temple precincts

The stone temple at Uley lay in the centre of a large settlement. It is known from the results of geophysical survey that stone buildings, and industrial activity, extended well north and east of the excavated area and a preliminary assessment of surface finds from the field west of the modern road indicated that stone buildings extended for at least 120 m (394 ft) in that direction. Only the ranges of buildings nearest to the temple were investigated during the excavation campaign (**30** and **31**). Each building was multi-phased and contained evidence for hearths, ovens, possible kilns and different flooring types, as well as varying groups of finds which could be taken as indicators to suggest functions for the various rooms and ranges. The stone structures had very substantial foundations, with wall bases rather thicker than those of the temple itself. Some of them may have been of two storeys and all were roofed with red sandstone tiles. By the later fourth century ancillary buildings were built with timber frames, while remnants of some of

the earlier stone structures were repaired and modified for reuse.

Reconstruction drawings of the excavated buildings are shown in **27** and are based on the plans of excavated structures devised for the different phases of occupation (see **31**). The courtyard is shown occupied by temporary booths and stalls set up for the selling of votive offerings to the pilgrims and, in the background, grazing goats occupy the pasture in front of the still venerated Neolithic tomb known as Hetty Pegler's Tump. Beyond, across the Severn estuary, the site of the Lydney temple might have been glimpsed. The reconstruction drawing has been based upon the excavated evidence of both plan and building materials, with some reference to reconstructions of similar buildings excavated at nearby Cirencester and the Frocester Court villa.

Building X was a major building, probably of two storeys, with two wings projecting southwards, a verandah surrounding the courtyard between them, and a focal room projecting northwards from the far elevation. Some elements of this plan are known only from aerial photographs. Structure I started its life as a simple rectangular suite of rooms and was extended several times. Structure IV was the corner of another large and multi-phased rectangular range of rooms, of unknown total dimensions. In comparison, Structure IX was a much more modest building, although this too was rebuilt and extended during its lifetime. Structures XIII and XIV were of timber construction, Structure XIII probably having been a wagon shed supported on sill beams, and Structure XIV a domestic structure with a hearth as well as porch of timber-framed construction.

Most known precinct buildings have been associated with isolated rural temples. At Colchester (Essex) the *temenos* of temple 6 included a second building interpreted as an assembly hall and at Pagan's Hill (Somerset) ranges of large rooms with long corridors or verandahs in front were laid out with a high degree of architectural sophistication. No specific functions could be ascribed to these buildings, but at Lydney it proved possible to define a major bath complex, associated with the healing cult of Nodens, a guesthouse or inn and a long building or *abaton* (**32**). The guesthouse presented a concise and regular plan with ranges of small rooms on three sides opening

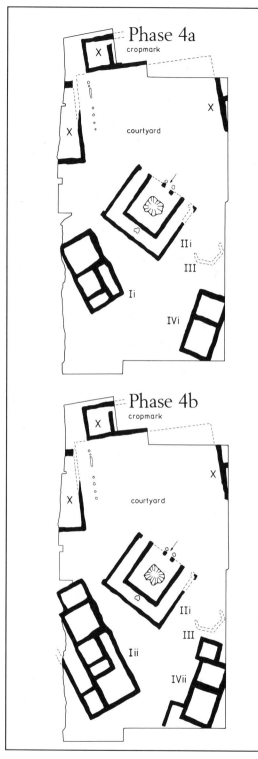

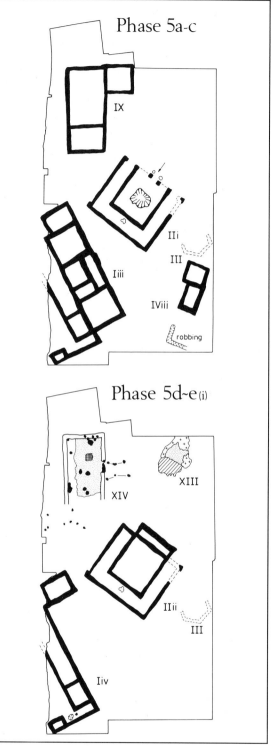

30 *Uley: layout of the temple area in the second and third centuries* AD.

31 *Uley: layout of the temple area in the early and mid-fourth century* AD.

through a verandah on to a central courtyard, and a forebuilding facing the temple itself on the fourth side. The small rooms were arranged in pairs and projecting from the centre of the rear range opposite the forebuilding was a larger focal room. With the exception of the forebuilding, the plan of this structure echoes that of Structure X at Uley, even to the presence of the focal projecting room, and it is suggested therefore that the latter may well also have functioned as a guesthouse and hostelry for visiting pilgrims. Wheeler's long building at Lydney comprised a range of eleven or more rooms, arranged in groups of three and opening on to a verandah behind the temple building. Mosaics were present throughout and there was evidence for three or four phases of repair and modification, the latest of which may have taken place in the post-Roman period. The building may have functioned as a row of shops selling votive offerings or served as a special suite for worshippers submitting themselves to sacred slumber, a necessary part of cults primarily concerned with healing. Thus at Lydney all three ancillary structures possessed very specialized functions.

Where temples were situated in more constricted situations in the midst of major rural settlements, the distinction between specialized and domestic buildings is much more difficult to define. At Wycomb (Glos.), excavated during the nineteenth century, a major settlement included a temple, and nearby, a row of simple one- or two-roomed rectangular buildings which may have been shops. But finally our attention must turn to the major complex at Nettleton (Wilts.) (**33** and see **25**). Here a major series of precinct structures has been assigned to three main phases of temple use and two phases of post-temple occupation. The structures ascribed an industrial function contained evidence for the working of iron or pewter. Otherwise identifications have been based either on position within the settlement: lodges next to the precinct gates and a 'priest's house' adjacent to the temple itself; or on plan type. Thus the large square building (11, replaced by 12) has been interpreted as a hostelry or guesthouse and the long narrow structure 10 near the temple has become the 'precinct shop'. In plan, most of the buildings at Nettleton are

reminiscent of the local form of farmhouse or barn typical of roadside settlements, as at Catsgore, Bradley Hill and Camerton, all in Somerset. In the absence of specific finds of recognized function from individual buildings it is difficult to assign any definite labels to the rectangular buildings at Nettleton.

The same conclusion must unfortunately also apply at Uley, although a few clues may be supplied by the finds distributions. With the exception of the proposed hostelry, Structure X, all other ancillary structures may be domestic in character, especially those which lie behind the temple itself. There may have been a further specialized building, but if so, its remains lie immediately east of the excavated area on the open side of the courtyard. The multi-phased rectangular buildings are best paralleled by local domestic and farm buildings, such as those excavated at Frocester Court and Barnsley Park, rather than with anything so exotic as the *abaton* at Lydney. However, this should not be surprising for it is only the elaboration of ritual associated with healing cults that requires the provision of several suites of buildings of special plan. At Uley the only large building needed may have been the guesthouse, for within a flourishing large rural

32 *Lydney: simplified plan of the temple precinct.*

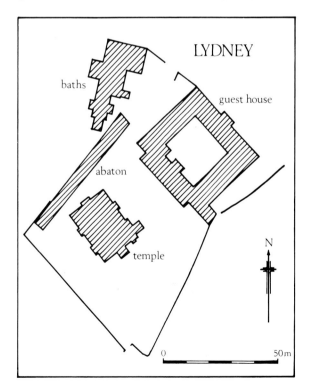

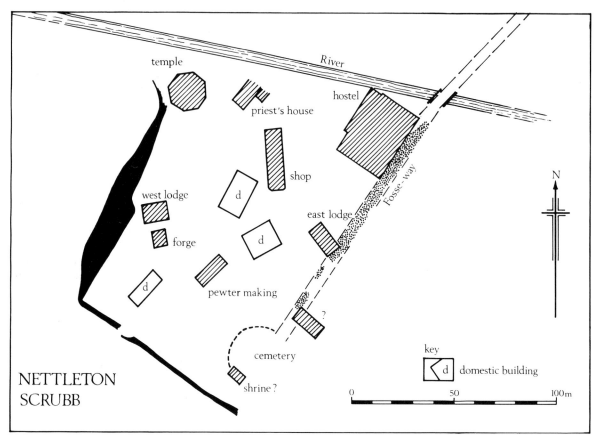

NETTLETON
SCRUBB

temple

priest's house

hostel

shop

west lodge

east lodge

forge

pewter making

cemetery

shrine?

River

Fosse-way

N

key

d domestic building

0   50   100m

settlement the commercial and marketing networks would have encompassed quite effortlessly the profitable trade in votive offerings, and the necessary movement of sacred goats from the grazing fields to the temple forecourt.

33 *Nettleton Scrubb: the temple and selected buildings in relation to the river, the boundary bank (shaded black), and the Roman road (Fosse Way).*

4

Belief and ritual

The popular concept of Celtic religion is dominated by the romantic vision of a long-haired Druid, enveloped in flowing white robes, peacefully enshrined in a leafy glade where he occupies himself in cutting mistletoe from a sacred oak tree. Whilst this simple generalized image of an Iron Age religious specialist has been discounted by modern scholars, certain elements of it may be authenticated in either classical sources or the archaeological record. We know that long hair and beards were the fashion amongst the Celtic aristocracy, although any flowing robes are more likely to have been of brown and blue woolly tartan rather than bleached. Also the officiant involved is quite likely to have been female. Sacred groves were certainly a preferred location for religious activities, and individual trees of particular species were held in special regard. However, the realm of offerings and sacrifices encompassed rather more than the cutting of magical branches, as will be seen in the next chapter.

It is difficult sometimes for our post-medieval minds to comprehend the strength and profundity of ancient beliefs and superstitions, which pervaded all aspects of everyday life to a powerful extent. As in many pre-industrial societies, pagan Celtic religion was dominated by the veneration of the natural. This ideology included particular respect for trees and greenery, animals and birds, and all watery places; it also involved identifiable elements of basic fertility ritual and totemism. The gods and goddesses worshipped were often associated with natural features and were believed to occupy a paradisical Otherworld. Places which were conceived as lying on the boundaries or interfaces between the known and other worlds

were regarded as particularly significant: islands at the edge of the land, large trees extending into the upper air space, and shafts or wells piercing the surface of the life-giving earth. Natural subjects imbued with supernatural powers were depicted in art in a lively, sophisticated and almost abstract style, in which beasts, birds, foliage and human heads were intertwined in magical combinations.

At the time of the conquest of Gaul and Britain, the fundamental aspects of Celtic religion were neither fully understood, nor approved of, by the Roman invaders. However, total eradication of the native beliefs was not seen to be desirable, even if it had been practicable, and most elements of Celtic belief and practice were absorbed within the complex system of pantheistic ritual which the Romans imported from the Mediterranean world. Some of the ways in which this absorption and transformation took place will be considered below. These changes reflected also the social and economic pressures of a time which saw the replacement of the collective, naturalistic and elemental beliefs of the pagan Celts by the overt materialism and individuality promoted by the urbanized Roman elite and the military machine.

The veneration of nature
Trees, foliage and groves fulfilled a central role in the pagan Celtic ideologies. Many sacred places were located in or adjacent to groves and, whilst Lucan's description of such a grove near Marseilles, where the gods were 'venerated with strange rites, the altars piled high with hideous offerings, and every tree was sprinkled with human blood', may include a note of exaggeration and outraged indignation,

the importance of such locations from southern France to Anglesey is well-attested in the classical sources. The Celtic place-name *nemeton*, related to the Greek word *temenos*, means grove, and in Britain several examples of such names may be associated with sacred places. The goddess worshipped at Buxton was Arnemetia, meaning 'she who dwelt over against the sacred grove', and the name of the nearest settlement to the religious centre on West Hill, Uley is Nympsfield, formerly *Nymdesfield*, meaning a tract of land belonging to a Celtic holy place, grove or shrine. The pagan timber temple at Uley was focused upon a series of

34 *Reconstruction of a stone dog sculpture from Pagan's Hill. The surviving fragments are 0.56 m (2 ft) high.*

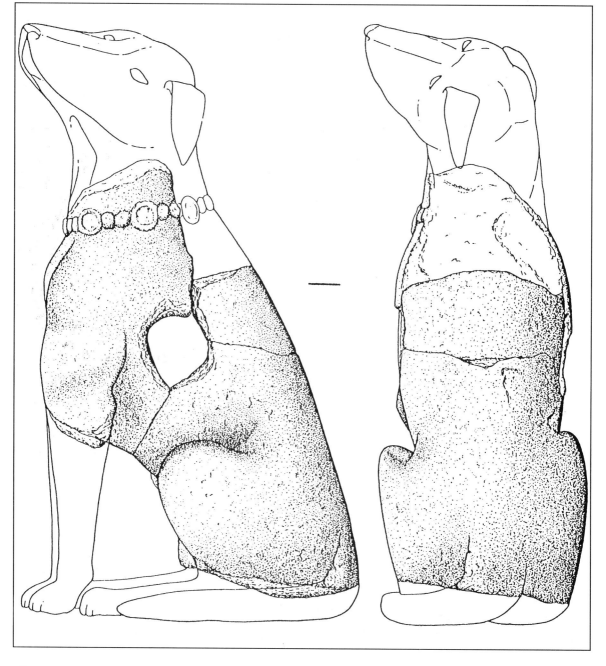

pits which may have held one or more sacred trees or wooden pillars. *Medionemeton*, 'the Middle Sanctuary', known to have existed near the Antonine Wall in Scotland, may have been located at Cairnpapple (West Lothian), where excavation of a Neolithic henge monument showed that this sacred spot continued to be revered in the Bronze Age and also in the Iron Age, when four humans were interred in long stone cists.

Whole tree trunks were sometimes placed in shafts, as at Swanwick (Hants.) and as depicted on the well-known silver cauldron, profusely decorated with Celtic and Oriental themes, found in a peat bog at Gundestrup in Denmark. Also, many idols were sculpted in wood. Whilst those surviving in waterlogged conditions tend to be small, larger examples carved from complete tree trunks probably existed. Such images may have occupied the massive post-sockets excavated within the long enclosure at Libenice (Czechoslovakia), for massive neck torcs were found lying nearby.

Foliage forms a major element of the contemporary art styles, and the provision of such embellishment around animal and human heads has given rise to the definition of a major motif, the 'leaf crown'. After the conquest, many sacred grove sites were respected but 'civilized' by the construction of Romano-Celtic temples. Thus the supernatural powers of the native sacred places were harnessed to celebrate the glory of Rome. Idols were generally replaced by images in stone but some elements of the leafy imagery survived, as in representations of one of the local Romano-Celtic deities of France, Erriapus, who was portrayed as a head emerging from foliage, as well as in the practice of offering decorated leaves of bronze or precious metal and the depiction of such leaves on altars and sculpture.

Watery places such as bogs, lakes and estuaries were regarded as liminal locations, situated at the very boundary of the Otherworld. As such they became repositories for the ritual deposition of valuable offerings. Strabo refers to great golden treasures which were kept both in temple-enclosures and secreted in the depths of sacred lakes near Toulouse, and the hoarding of deposits in rivers, bogs and lakes formed a frequent characteristic of European Celtic societies from at least the later Bronze Age. Whilst this type of ritual hoarding does not appear to have continued into Roman times,

perhaps because by then individuals were too well aware of the material value of their prized personal possessions, the veneration of springs and wells increased dramatically. This was probably connected with the substantial growth of cults connected with healing, and in Britain is well exemplified by the remarkable development of religious establishments at Bath, Lydney, Coventina's Well, and, probably, at Nettleton. As we shall see, such healing water cults were often associated with the veneration of sculpted human heads or skulls, but representations of dogs (Lydney, Pagan's Hill (**34**) and Coventina's Well) or the ram (Bath) were typical also. In many cases, these cult centres were established on the sites of significant Iron Age shrines or groves, but little detailed evidence for their structure or function has survived.

The importance of shafts and wells as contexts for ritual deposits has been highlighted by Anne Ross, and the British evidence has been analysed in detail by Gerald Wait. In the Iron Age, all known examples derive from southern England, with a particular concentration in Kent and Surrey. The deposits generally comprised cattle and human bones, pottery vessels and ash, whilst those in the south-east were particularly characterized by the bones of birds and dogs. Such deposits reflected the Celtic ritual emphasis on fertility and the natural world. In the Roman period, deliberate deposition within shafts and wells became more widespread and the variety of items deposited increased. New categories included tools, votive objects, pig bones, oysters and coins. Deposition of human bones and ash, however, became rare and was limited to civilian sites, whilst shafts in the military zones tended to contain querns, pieces of armour and weapons. Such changes can be seen to reflect the growing concepts of personal wealth and the individual that typified the development of Romanized society.

Animals and birds held a central position in Celtic conceptions of the supernatural and figured extensively in the art of the period. Bulls, boars and horses were associated with war and hunting, as were the antlers and horns which often adorned the heads of humans or animals alike in decorative schemes. Composite beasts such as the ram-headed snake were also commonly represented. But all-powerful were selected species of birds such as the soaring

35 *Incised representation of an eagle on a bone plaque from Lydney.*

36 *Stylized outline of a goose, carved on a slab from Easterton of Roseisle, Moray.*

supreme eagle (**35**); water-birds connected with fertility and healing; the goose representing the destructive forces of aggression and magic (**36**); and, above all, the crow and the crane which were seen as mysterious agents of the Otherworld, heralds of death and the signs of evil power. The Romans absorbed some of these traditions, but with the exception of the eagle, symbol of divine imperial strength, and the use of flight patterns in prophecy, the dominance of birds gave way to the elevation of animal symbols. These tended to include domestic species and, together with chickens and cockerels, they came to be associated with particular gods or goddesses (**37** and **38**). Thus the central role of animals and birds in Celtic belief became 'humanized' and took on a subsidiary position in relation to the mighty deities of the Roman world.

The cult of the head
No single aspect of Celtic iconography has attracted such wide-ranging discussion as the cult of the disembodied or severed human head. However, cults involving human crania and depictions of heads in stone or other materials were not an innovation of the Iron Age period in Europe. The importance of skulls in the ancestor cults known from the long barrows of Neolithic Britain is echoed by the symbolic representations of faces amongst the motif repertoire of megalithic art, and in the round on such objects as the late Neolithic decorated chalk drums from Folkton Wold, Yorkshire.

More realistic sculptures of heads include the remarkable schematic representations in sandstone from the Early Neolithic site of Lepenski Vir in Yugoslavia, while hints of veneration of the human head in more distant realms of the past are evidenced by the groups of decorated human skulls found deliberately deposited in a cave at Ofnet in southern Germany by Mesolithic hunters of the immediate post-glacial era. Thus from early times the human head appears to have been regarded not only as the seat of human intellect and the essence of being, but also as a symbol of supernatural powers.

Severed human heads are a common motif in Celtic art and iconography on the European continent and, indeed, Anne Ross believes that 'the human head is given first place as being the most typical Celtic religious symbol'. The clearest manifestations of the cult are found in the south of France, where the great shrine of Entremont was embellished with sculptures depicting piles of human heads and by the actual crania of warriors nailed to the wall.

37 *Copper alloy goat from Uley (h. 2.5 cm (1 in)).*

38 *Copper alloy cockerel from Uley (h. 2.4 cm (1 in)).*

The architectural scheme of the portico belonging to a similar temple at Roquepertuse included niches which, once again, were set with human skulls. The placing of the heads of distinguished enemies in temples like these is mentioned by classical authors such as Diodorus Siculus, Strabo and Livy who refer also to the embalming of severed heads in cedar oil, in order that they could be used for conspicuous and dramatic display. However, such positive evidence for a head cult is not forthcoming from Britain. In a recent survey, Gerald Wait has expressed the opinion that no convincing evidence for the pre-Roman cult of the head can be found north of the Massif Central. Even the skulls fallen from stakes above the gates of the hillforts at Bredon Hill (Hereford and Worcs.) and Stanwick (Yorkshire) are regarded by him as representing war trophies in a civil or secular context, rather than as possessing any religious connotations. On the other hand, human heads do occur on objects and utensils decorated in the Celtic style in Britain, and

this aspect of the Celtic ideology cannot be said to have been totally absent from the insular Iron Age. Perhaps the most remarkable of the head motifs from southern England are those depicted on the Marlborough vat, which are reminiscent of the heads shown on many late Iron Age coins, and the more traditionally styled handle attachments on the bucket from Aylesford, which display the staring lentoid eyes and expressionless lips which are characteristic of many continental representations of the human face.

In the Roman period, the Celtic continental tradition of veneration of the head was intensified by the classical concept of representing the heads of specific individuals, mainly in the context of the accurate portraiture of ancestors in two or three dimensions. A very large number of cult heads in stone are known from Roman Britain. Their formal characteristics and their geographical concentration in the northern counties have been described in detail by Anne Ross. Many of the heads are stray finds and

39 *Copper alloy plaque of Apollo from Nettleton Scrubb (actual size).*

40 *Two copper alloy masks from Coventina's Well, probably used to decorate buckets or cauldrons. One (left) displays Celtic features; the other is more classical in style.*

cannot be dated unequivocally to the Roman period, but among those from excavated contexts are the stone head with prominent eyeballs in oval outlines and a straight nose from the floor of a Roman shrine at Caerwent. Such stone heads were designed to be set in or against architectural features. More mobile would have been the face masks, manufactured in metal, which are another common manifestation of the head cult in Roman Britain. One of the most famous of these, and certainly one of the largest, is the tin mask found in the culvert of the sacred spring at Bath in 1878. The grooved hair and elongated straight nose are again in a native Celtic style and the eyes are represented by sockets which were once filled, probably with glass. Martin Henig has suggested that this mask may have been fixed to the head of a votive image executed otherwise in wood. Other masks from religious sites in Britain tend to be smaller and include the depiction in native style on a copper alloy plaque from Nettleton of the bust and head of Apollo (**39**). The eyes are now hollow, but once would have been filled with glass or enamel. Although in this case the inscription above the head identifies it to be that of a major deity, other examples were probably not so intended and may have been medical ex-votos or generalized votives imbued with the supreme power of the head. Amongst recently published examples there are two typical small masks from Coventina's Well on Hadrian's Wall (**40**). One possesses lentoid eyes, a long triangular nose and downturned mouth, in typical Celtic style, whilst the other displays a more classical treatment,

with full cheeks, a small mouth and a Romanized hairstyle. Although both masks may have originated as mounts on buckets or pieces of furniture, it does seem likely that they came to be deposited within the well as votive offerings. This use of the significant parts of objects as ritual offerings recalls the apparently intentional dismemberment of figurines and statues to provide medical or other ex-votos which will be mentioned later. Often it was the head of the image that was selected for secondary use. Further evidence concerning the importance attached to the head of metal figurines has been observed in relation to two recently studied figurines. In the case of the Celtic, and probably Iron Age, figure of a female from Henley Wood (**41**), it is the face that has been worn most by handling, and the same observation applies to one of the figurines of Mercury from Uley. It seems that the greatest power was perceived to reside in the face of the image, and that this power was believed to be transferable by touch.

Celtic and Roman deities

Differences between the basic beliefs of the Iron Age and Romano-British populations may be investigated by comparing the gods and goddesses worshipped in the Celtic and Roman worlds. Such a comparison is complicated by the regional, as opposed to purely functional, character of many of the Celtic deities and by the fact that we know relatively little of the names and detailed roles of the pre-Roman gods and goddesses. The characteristics of the major members of the Roman pantheon are well understood, along with their particular items of clothing, accoutrements and appropriate equipment or animal associates. From inscriptions in Gaul, some named Celtic gods may be matched against Roman equivalents but a full listing or description of the pre-Roman deities cannot be attained. In order to present a summary of the very complex picture of belief and worship, which has formed the subject matter of many full-length books, the deities have been divided here into five major groups. The initial two groups comprise deities primarily concerned with firstly the natural world and fertility and secondly with powers of healing. These groups were supreme in the Celtic world and continued to have an important role in the Roman period.

41 *Copper alloy figurine of a female deity from Henley Wood (actual size 7.75 cm (3 in)).*

However, the Roman system of religion developed and subtly transformed some aspects of veneration and spheres of interest with the evolution of three new categories of deities. These were connected with the concept of pre-eminent male and female deities; aggression and hunting; and the very important subjects of prosperity, travel and trade. All these new departures were connected with the increasing importance of the individual personality, and the crucial role of individual economic performance, within Roman society.

The main deities connected with the Celtic worship of the natural world and fertility were the generalized mother-goddess, the gods later identified in Gaul with a conflated Mars/Mercury figure, and more specific individual ones such as the horned woodland god Cernunnos, and Epona, goddess of corn and fruit, dogs and horses. Associated with these nature gods were certain animal attributes, in particular the ram-headed snake. In the Roman world a widespread fertility cult was commonly represented by the veneration of Venus, including the Pseudo-Venus and Dea Nutrix forms, the Deae Matres and Cupid, whilst woodland and agriculture were linked with deities such as Silvanus and Ceres. The other main sphere of worship in the Celtic world related to healing. The deities connected with this aspect were usually of a local and individual nature, such as Sulis, Nodens or Coventina, connected with the major watery healing centres at Bath, Lydney and Carrawburgh respectively. Certain animals, especially dogs, and disembodied heads or skulls were also related to these cults, whilst in Gaul the local versions of Hercules seem to have possessed specific powers of healing. In Roman times many Celtic centres of healing were adopted and developed, and the name of the Celtic deity amplified by the addition of a respectable Roman deity such as Minerva at Bath, or Apollo at Nettleton.

In the Roman world, deities connected with personal aggression and hunting became more common. Diana, the hunting goddess, Vulcan with his hammer and tools, and the classical Hercules carrying his club, are common examples, but the supreme candidate is Mars, the god of war, characterized by his helmet and different categories of votive weapon. The classical concept of individual power was demonstrated by the worship of one supreme male, Jupiter, and the chief goddess, Minerva,

as well as through the Imperial cult (**42** and **43**). Finally, the economic prowess of the Roman empire was guided and protected by the worship of *Genii Cucullati* – little gods of riches and prosperity – their local and household versions and, above all, by the ubiquitous cult of Mercury, patron of merchants, travel, trade and crafts. Characterized by his winged helmet, boots and *caduceus*, he was associated with the cockerel, ram or goat, and the tortoise (see **37**, **38** and **47**).

The relative importance of the different deities in Roman Britain may be demonstrated by a consideration of the incidence of depictions of identifiable gods and goddesses from different sites. In **44** the occurrence of images in stone or bronze from a series of sites in midland and southern Britain has been summarized. The sites selected include five Roman towns, four rural temple sites and one cache of figurines (from Southbroom in Wiltshire). It should be noted that the urban data includes finds from temples and other locations within the towns, as listed by Miranda Green. It can be seen that six deities occur most commonly, with Mercury by far the most widespread. Second place is held by Venus, goddess of fertility, followed by the gods of war and aggression, Hercules and Mars, and then by the supreme goddess, Minerva. A similar pattern was deduced by Miranda Green's study of all the religious material from civilian Roman Britain, the only significant difference being that Jupiter also occurred in her six most commonly represented deities. Thus the replacement of the elemental Celtic cults concerned with nature and healing by the materialistic and self-centred ideologies of the Roman world is demonstrated in the archaeological record.

Most Roman temples would have contained a large cult image representing the main deity worshipped at the shrine. These have seldom survived as they would have been stolen, smashed or melted down when the temples were dismantled or destroyed. The most impressive example from Britain is from Uley (**colour plate 2** and see **7**), where, using the mutilated fragments of a larger than life statue that had been concealed within later Christian buildings on the site, it has been possible to attempt a reconstruction of the cult figure. As Martin Henig has shown, the statue was of high quality and based on a prototype of the later classical period, probably by Praxiteles. The only non-classical element is the use of a local stone; the stance, musculature and tooling of the surviving portions are purely classical, while the treatment of the curls and eyes recall early Roman works of the Mediterranean world. The figures of ram and cockerel are small in relation to the figure of Mercury – a common artistic device which served to augment the power and supremacy of the god. That similar statues in stone or copper alloy existed in other temples is hinted at by the discovery of isolated detached heads, of life, or larger than life, size, such as those of Hadrian from London, Claudius from the river near Colchester, and a gilded Minerva, recovered from a sewer trench in Bath. Some cult statues may have been of wood, embellished with metal masks and accoutrements, and most images would have been richly coloured with paint and enamels. Use of wood echoes the widespread use of wooden idols in Celtic Europe; many of these having been preserved in the springs and lakes where they were deposited. Occasional earlier images of stone have also been recovered, including the

42 *Small bust of Jupiter from Uley, probably an ornamental fitting (actual size 3 cm (1¼ in)).*

43 *Copper alloy figurine of Minerva, goddess of war, from Lamyatt (actual size).*

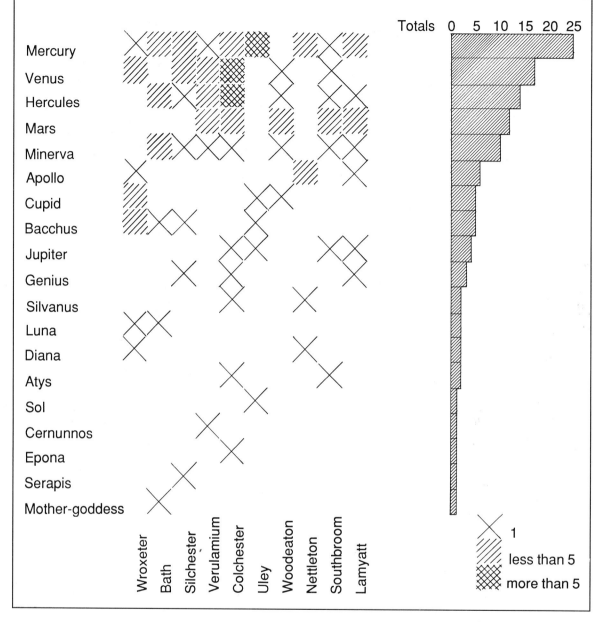

44 *The occurrence of depictions of deities, in stone or bronze, in five urban and five rural locations.*

Early Iron Age statue which probably surmounted a large family burial mound at Hirschlanden in Germany (**45**). The power radiated by the figure is not dissimilar to that invested in the great cult statues of the Roman world, although the helmet, neck torc and Hallstatt dagger, along with the summary treatment of the physiognomy, firmly place this image in its Celtic context.

Much more commonly found than the cult statues are small images and figurines of Roman deities cast in copper alloy. British examples have been catalogued by Miranda Green and recent excavations have led to the recovery of several groups of such figurines, notably from Lamyatt Beacon and Uley. The styles of these more everyday offerings may be indicative of underlying cultural leanings amongst the

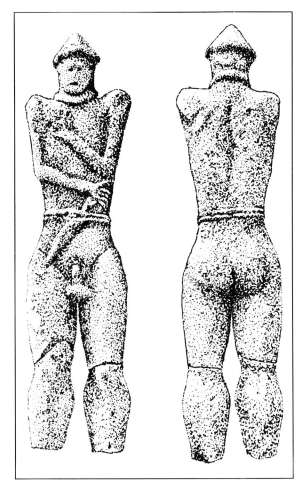

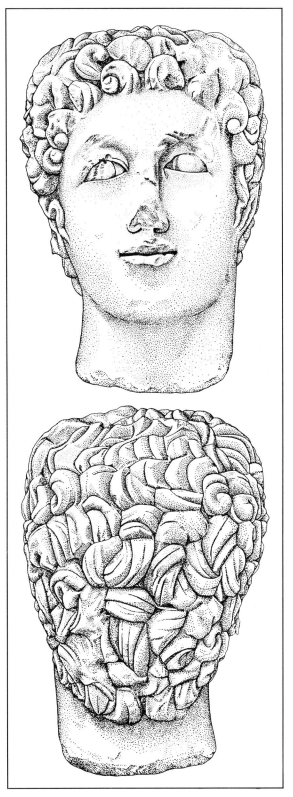

45 *Stone statue which probably surmounted a burial mound of Early Iron Age date at Hirschlanden in Germany (actual size: 1.5 m (5 ft) high).*

46 *Head of a stone statue of Mercury from Uley (slightly larger than life size).*

native populace and it is instructive to compare a series of depictions of a single god, Mercury, from the temples of Uley and Lamyatt (see **46** to **49**). Two are in strong classical style – one naked and reminiscent of the great Uley cult statue (**47**), and one wearing cloak and winged helmet (**48**). Both adopt elegant poses and possess carefully executed formal hairstyles with curls (compare **46** and **colour plate 2**). In contrast, the second figurine from Uley, which superficially occupies the form of a nude classical image, has a stiff and stilted appearance; the helmet and money bag are summarily treated

and the hair is indicated by rough vertical strokes. These features reflect the more stylized and dehumanized approach of the Celtic artist, and this is even more pronounced in the case of the bucket mount from Uley (**49**), where the face of the deity, flanked by sinuous scrolls, has been reduced to staring lentoid eyes, a simple triangular nose and straight mouth. The hair is represented by crude strokes and the wings of the Mercurial helmet are reduced to vestigial knobbed projections or horns. Such items of native manufacture are much more common in western and northern Britain than in the south-east and suggest a considerable survival of Celtic culture and workmanship beneath the veneer of Romanization.

Styles of worship

A significant difference between the patterns of worship practised by the Celts and Romans is well represented by the contrasts in the ritual buildings employed. In the Celtic Iron Age, shrines, where they existed at all, were very

47 *Copper alloy figurine of Mercury from Uley (actual size).*

48 *Copper alloy figurine of Mercury from Lamyatt (actual size).*

small and acted as foci for predominantly open-air rituals linked with watery places or sylvan groves. Roman religion was practised in imposing architectural edifices, temples, which were far larger and more flamboyant than their mysterious Celtic counterparts. The temples were large enough for at least some of the congregation to enter the building, although, as in the Iron Age, much of the ritual, sacrifice and feasting would have been enacted in the open. In both the Iron Age and Roman periods, male and female specialists presided over the worship, and undertook divination and sacrifice; parts of the animals sacrificed were eaten subsequently during ritual feasts.

Whilst the major Celtic festivals were closely related to events of the agricultural year, the Roman religious calendar was much more complex and centred more on the veneration of individual gods and goddesses. The Roman Lupercalia of mid-February carried on some of

49 *Copper alloy bucket mount from Uley with Mercury in native style (twice actual size).*

the features of the great Celtic farming festival of Imbolc, and the Parilia (21 April) and Floralia (28 April to 3 May) included elements formerly included in the fertility and purification rituals of the May Day Beltaine. However, the Roman harvest was celebrated rather later than the Celtic feast of Lughnasa, while the great Celtic festival of the supernatural, Samain (31 October and 1 November) appears to have been suppressed.

Little detail concerning Celtic rituals can be deduced from archaeological evidence but more material is available for the Roman period. Decorated sacrificial weapons and tools have been identified, and specialist implements and utensils for the presentation and serving of offerings at the sacrificial feasts. These include sets of pewter and metal vessels, such as those recovered recently from the sacred spring at Bath: paterae, strainers and spoons. A sense of

50 *Iron candle holders from Lydney (left and centre) and Uley (right).*

the dramatic was carefully engineered by the use of linked architectural spaces within interiors, and by the subtle lighting of cult figures. Such lighting effects were achieved by the careful positioning of window openings and the use of lamps and candles (**50**). The earthly abode of the gods was rendered fragrant by the use of incense, which may have been burnt on special clay vessels such as those found at Coventina's Well (**51**) and now known also from Uley. In addition, herbs and spices may have been scattered on the sacrificial altars and hearths; a kind of supernatural barbecue. Ethereal sounds would have been provided by the use of rattles, tambourines, cymbals and bells, taking over the very powerful role of the Celtic harp and its provision of gentle music which was believed to echo the sweetness of the Otherworld. Similarly, the chanting of hymns would have stimulated a sense of inner awareness of the divine presence. No doubt such states were also promoted by the employment of sedatives and hallucinogenic drugs.

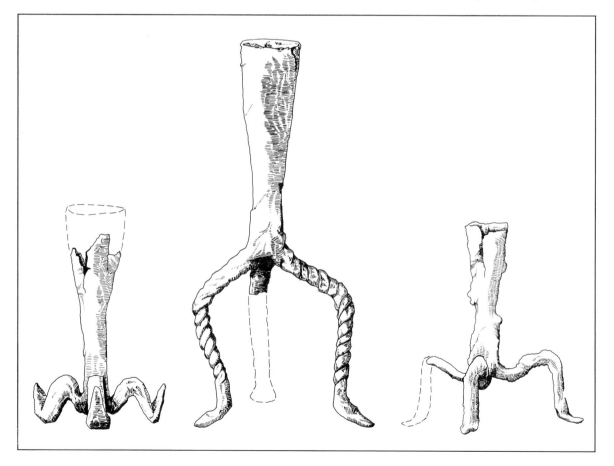

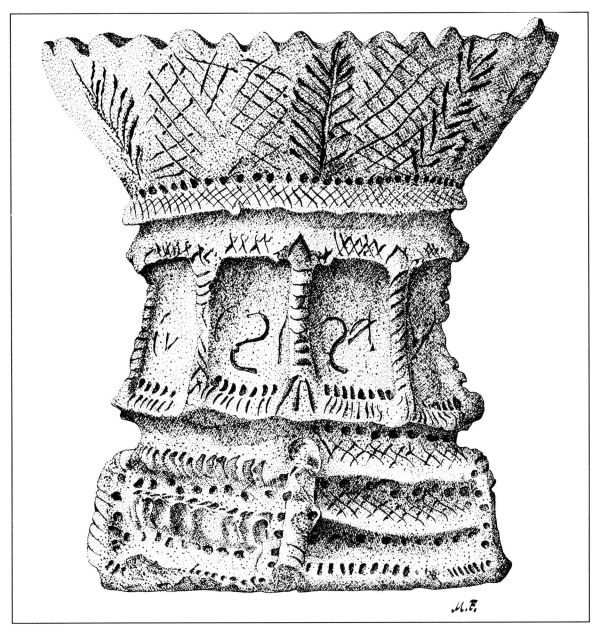

51 *Baked clay incense burner from Coventina's Well. The decoration consists mainly of palm leaves and cross-hatching, while the inset panels bear the letters of an inscription: the name of the person who offered the object.*

Some of these effects are illustrated in the hypothetical reconstruction of the interior of the Romano-Celtic temple at Uley (**colour plate 3**). Carefully contrived lighting effects achieved by high-placed windows and low level lamps and candles will have provided dramatic highlighting to the main, larger than life-size, cult figure. This statue could be observed, with suitable awe and wonder, only from a prescribed distance. Priests made offerings at the internal altars, the smoke mingling with the aroma of incense as it rose to the heights of the central cella roof, while a worshipper approached to offer up a humble gift to the supreme god Mercury.

65

5

Offerings and sacrifice

Priests and people would have gathered at the sites of shrines and other holy places to worship their gods, to celebrate the prescribed feasts and festivals, to ask favours, and to offer up suitable gifts and sacrifices. Where the physical remains of these offerings or sacrifices became buried, either deliberately or by accident, then objects have been preserved for discovery by archaeological techniques. Thus we have, at least from some of the shrines, some hard evidence from which patterns of offerings and categories of sacrifice can be reconstructed. This evidence usually consists of small objects made from metal, stone or bone, and sometimes baked clay; larger items of sculpted stone, such as altars, and organic remains such as wood, nuts or bones. The bones derived from living sacrifices may belong to either animals or humans and may occur as complete skeletons, partial bodies or heaps of mixed bones representing the debris from the mass butchery of victims or the waste from ritual feasts. The incidence of specific object types chosen as offerings, and the categories of sacrifice, changed through time and those current in the Iron Age period contrast to some extent with those of the Roman period.

Iron Age offerings

Eight of the Iron Age shrine sites described in Chapter 2 have produced groups of finds that can be interpreted as having religious connotations. These items include the remains of human and animal bodies, which will be discussed later in the chapter, and objects of metal such as coins, weapons, jewellery and horse trappings, along with a few instances of tools and ceramic vessels. Celtic coins of gold, silver and bronze have been found at Harlow, Hayling Island, Maiden Castle, Thistleton, Uley and Woodeaton. Such coins were valuable items in the Celtic economy and their distribution reflected the spheres of influence of a series of wealthy and influential tribal leaders. At Harlow more than 200 such coins have been recovered, over half of them from layers sealed beneath the stone foundations and levels associated with the Roman temple. A group of gold coins was concentrated under the exact area of the later temple and two clusters of bronze coins were found just to the south. The coins may have been individually suspended either within timber shrines or from wooden carved figures or totem poles. Alternatively they possibly may have been concealed in bags or containers of perishable material such as wood, cloth or leather, either again hanging or buried in the earth. A slightly smaller assemblage of Celtic coins was found at Hayling Island; gold and silver coins were not present here and it seems that the most valuable items had been removed in antiquity. However, the remaining examples were still of high value and there was a large proportion of coins that had at some time been brought over from Gaul (now France).

Almost as common as the deposits of coins on these Iron Age shrine sites was the occurrence of weapons. These included full-sized, functional weapons such as the remarkable series of bolt- and spearheads found in the shrine and votive pit at Uley (**52**) and small models representing weapons on some other sites. At Worth (Kent) there were three miniature shields and at Woodeaton four axes and six small spears, all manufactured from copper alloy. The next most numerous class of votive material was jewellery, usually in the form of copper alloy brooches. These occurred at Harlow, Maiden Castle, Thistleton and Worth. In addition, in the shrine area at South Cadbury a pendant decorated with two ducks' heads was found. Of more than 50 brooches of pre-Roman type found at Harlow, 27 were sealed in the pre-temple Iron Age deposits. They were mainly of the simple safety-pin type where bow, spring and pin were cast all in one piece. The bow was often decorated with cast ribs, rows of punch marks or beaded ridges. Metal objects associated with horse harness or carts and chariots appear to have been significant on at least two sites. At Hayling Island examples of horse and chariot fittings were associated with 17 spearheads, belt hooks, two decorated strap links, several pieces of sword scabbards and two bronze standard handles. The main groups of finds from Late Iron Age levels near the pre-Roman circular shrine included fine pottery, 15 brooches of early type, various iron weapons, six Celtic coins and some harness fittings along with the bones of a pony. Finally there are a few instances of more everyday items associated with shrine sites: the unusual antler and bone heavy tools and partially preserved pots with pierced bases from the pit at Uley; and the finding of several iron currency bars, which functioned as ingots or simple units for barter, in the courtyard at Hayling Island.

Roman votive objects

In the Roman period the deposition of both coins and occasional tools or pots continued, as did the offering of metal weapons. However, the carrying of weapons by civilians was now against the law, and only items of miniature size were now employed. Jewellery and other personal items continued as a popular form of offering but were joined by two new major categories of ritual object: firstly items that were designed purely for votive use; and secondly, various objects bearing inscriptions revering, or seeking requests from, a particular deity.

Totals of over 8000 and nearly 3000 coins survived to be excavated by archaeologists at Lydney and Uley respectively and, from a small portion of the churned-up deposits remaining in the sacred spring at Bath, more than 12,000 have been recovered. Statistical study of these and other coin groups from sacred sites has suggested that in general the proportions represented through time are similar to the

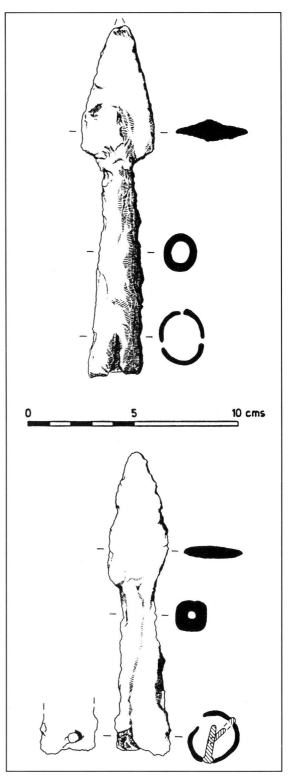

52 *Iron spearheads from the votive pit at Uley.*

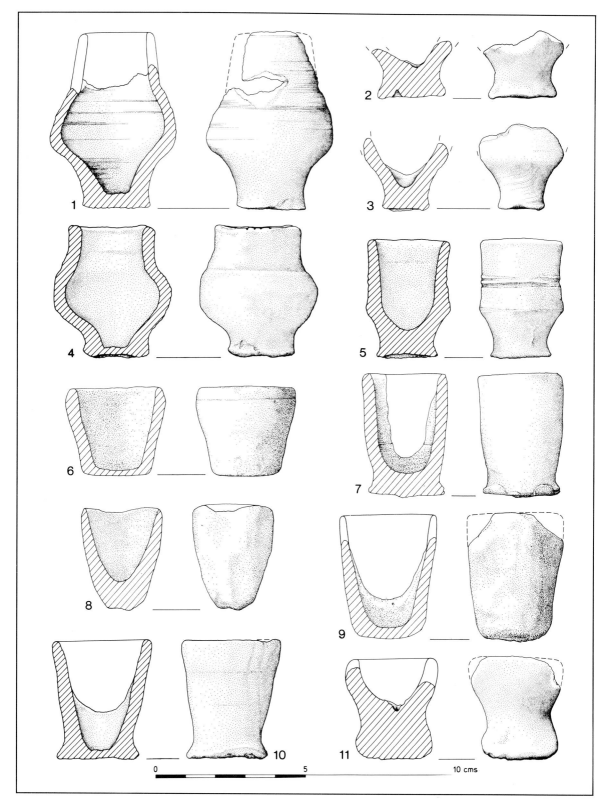

0   5   10 cms

patterns detected at other rural sites of a more domestic nature, but contrast markedly in some ways with the coin lists obtained for excavated major towns. The reasons for these variations are not yet clear, and the only significant characteristic of religious assemblages that can be detected is the high incidence of forgeries and 'copies', coins which mimicked certain mid-fourth-century prototypes, on temple sites. Thus *Fel Temp Reparatio* copies, bearing on the reverse the inscription *Fel(icium) Temp(orum) Reparatio* ('the return of happier times'), were extremely common at Uley and copies of ever decreasing size, known therefore as *minims* and *minimissimi*, were a major component in the votive assemblage from Lydney. As well as these copies of particular regular coinage there were also found items that could be interpreted as 'ring money', various forms of metal rings which may have been employed as a divine currency. Simple iron or bronze rings are fairly common on temple sites, as are finger rings also, and at Uley a series of copper alloy rings designed to be viewed from one side only, were both apparently manufactured and sold to the pilgrims, on the temple site.

As mentioned above, votive weapons in the Roman period were represented only by miniatures. Axes and spears were the most common categories and they might be made from copper alloy, iron or silver and sometimes were embell-

53 *(Left) Miniature clay vessels from Uley.*

54 *An enamelled brooch from Lamyatt in the form of a horse and rider. Such brooches may be associated with the cult of Mars, god of war. Vertical shading denotes red enamel; horizontal shading blue (height: 3 cm (1¼ in)).*

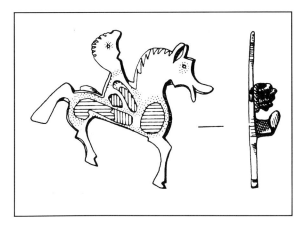

ished with inscriptions or ritual signs such as crosses or swastikas. Model spears from Uley and Woodeaton had been bent double in an act of ritual damage or breakage. This practice is clearly demonstrated in the case of the fine silver spear from Uley with its elegant twisted shaft and pierced blade (**colour plate 4**). Various full-sized pieces of equipment and tools are known from temple sites. These include querns, whetstones, spindlewhorls, styli (for writing on wax or inscribing metal), woodworking tools and knives. They appear to be domestic in function but some, especially the knives and styli, may have been used for votive and sacrificial purposes. Some types of pottery or other baked clay items are more specific in design: clay lamps and incense burners, hollow stands for lamps or containers, and miniature pots (**53**). These miniature vessels are known now from a series of temple sites including Verulamium, Silchester (*insula* VII), Coleshill and Uley. Among over a hundred such pots retrieved at Uley, a few copied the shapes of full-size beakers (**53**, 1 to 5), but most were simple thumb pots with or without irregular pedestal bases.

As in the Iron Age, items of jewellery were a common offering, and initially brooches were the most popular choice. Most were of the style generally in fashion but a few seem to have belonged to groups that were particularly manufactured for religious and votive use. One such group of brooches depicted horses and riders, often decorated with brightly-coloured enamel inlay (**54**). As well as at Lamyatt Beacon, they also occur on five other religious sites including Hayling Island, Woodeaton and Hockwold (Norfolk), a site which also produced a group of ritual metal crowns. Such horseman brooches could be associated with a warrior cult, although the riders depicted are not equipped with weapons. As the Roman period developed, and fashions in jewellery changed, the items offered up at the temples also varied. Pins, finger rings and bracelets were now the most common finds, but necklaces of glass beads, pendants, chains and ear-rings are also well represented. The jewellery was made from various raw materials. Silver or copper alloy, bone or antler, shale and jet were the most common, and individual pieces were often embellished with enamel, semi-precious stones or a mosaic of *millefiori* glass. The range and diversity of such material is demonstrated by an array of

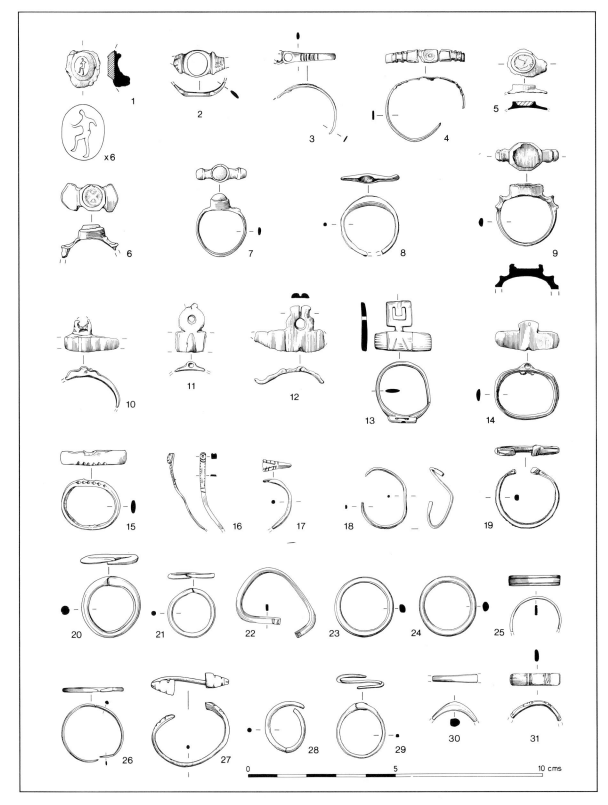

finger rings (**55**), some of silver (nos. 14, 16, 23, 24 and 25), some with plain or engraved glass stones (nos. 2, 5, 6, 7 and 8), and one a signet ring with a fine intaglio of a satyr. Others are simple overlapping rings, possibly akin to the ring money described above, while another series (nos. 10 to 14) are key-rings with projecting devices that may have opened the locks to boxes or chests.

Of the radically new categories of votive object introduced during the Roman period the most noteworthy are the copper alloy figurines of gods and goddesses, discussed in the previous chapter, and items, usually of stone or sheet metal, bearing specific inscriptions of a religious nature. The bronze plaque of Apollo from Nettleton (see **39**) is a fine example of this type of material. In recent years, however, a major development has been the discovery of two large groups of inscribed lead sheets, 130 from the sacred spring at Bath and a further 140 from the votive rubbish deposits at Uley. These inscribed tablets are commonly known as 'curses' because they often bear a message to the god requesting the pursuit of vengeance against an enemy. This enemy had usually offended by stealing a piece of property; property which could vary in face value from a piece of clothing or draught animal to a beloved wife. Often the invocations were composed using set formulas reminiscent of legal phrases, as if to provide them with authority and respectability, but detailed study of the handwriting has suggested that they were written by many

55 (Left) Finger rings from Uley. No. 1 (of iron) contains a glass intaglio bearing the figure of a satyr. Nos. 14, 16, 23, 24, and 25 are of silver; the rest are of copper alloy.

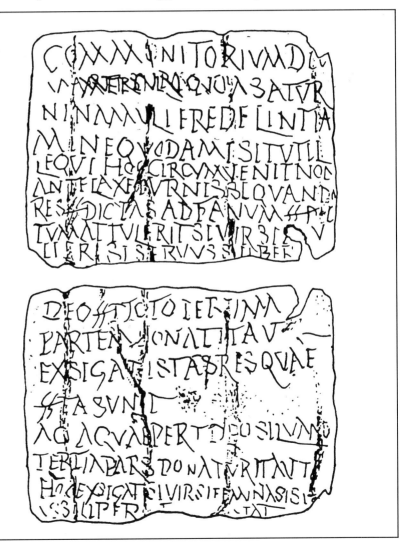

56 (Right) Lead sheet from Uley bearing an inscription to Mercury on both sides. The sheet was tightly rolled when found and has been carefully unfolded in the laboratory (actual size).

hands and not by one or two specialists. A clear example of a curse from Uley is shown in **56**. It reads: 'A reminder to the God Mercury ['Mars-Silvanus' erased] from Saturnina, a woman, concerning the linen cloth she has lost. Let him who stole it have not rest until he brings the aforesaid things to the aforesaid temple, whether this is a man or woman, slave or free' and, continuing on the reverse: 'She gives a third part to the aforesaid god on condition that he exact those things which have been aforewritten. A third part of what has been lost is given to the god Silvanus on condition that he exact this, whether [the criminal?] is a man or woman, slave or free.' Other curses are rather more bloodthirsty, with requests for the god to attack the enemy's heart, liver, lungs, intestines, veins and marrow, or their very mind, memory and thoughts.

Other new types of votive object employed in the Roman period are sheet alloy leaves or feathers and copper alloy letters. The letters were often pierced and presumably were used to compose the names of deities or entire inscriptions which could be nailed to a wooden board or to the fabric of the temple itself. The stylized sheet-metal leaves or feathers are roughly triangular in shape and decorated with a representation of veining executed by incision or the repoussé technique. In addition, they sometimes bore a depiction of a god or goddess and, occasionally, a punched inscription. Some may have adorned priestly head-dresses or other items of clothing but most functioned probably as votive objects in their own right. They appear to have been a highly valued category of material, some being provided with a shiny tinned or silvered surface.

The patterning of offerings

Before comparing some of the larger temple assemblages in detail it is necessary to say a few words concerning the nature of these groups of finds. Firstly, the finds that survive are those that have been sealed and protected from later disturbance. In some cases, such as Brean Down, few votive objects other than coins were recovered and it seems likely that all valuables were removed at the time of desertion or demolition. In other cases, certain groups of finds were hidden in pits or became sealed by falls of masonry. Finally, and very fortunately for the archaeologist, in a few instances major heaps or other deposits of votive material

became buried and forgotten in or around the temple buildings so that a very large collection of objects survived for the excavator to rediscover. This had happened at Lydney, Uley, Coventina's Well, and, to some extent, at Nettleton. Another aspect of the finds groups that needs emphasizing is that the composition of the types within the assemblage would have varied through time. Often the lack of stratification has not allowed this subject to be considered fully, but at Uley some general conclusions could be drawn. In the first century AD tools and pottery formed a significant component of the votive assemblages. These categories included heavy tools manufactured from bone and antler, and almost complete ceramic vessels, several of which possessed groups of holes drilled through the lower wall or base. Full-sized weapons were also being ritually deposited, along with a few coins and brooches. Full-sized tools or weapons were not used as votives from the second century onwards and, during the main *floruit* of the stone temple the most popular forms seem to have been miniature clay vessels, coins, antler pins, spoons and toilet articles. As the Roman period progressed, items of jewellery were more commonly deposited, especially bracelets, glass beads and finger rings, and these were accompanied by copper alloy figurines, miniature weapons, sheet-metal plaques and leaves, metal vessels and the 'ring money' described previously.

It is likely that objects of particular value or complexity at Uley would have been guarded carefully and reused several times. Thus some of the figurines deposited in the fourth century probably began their ritual life in the second. Amongst the simpler objects certain trends through time can be deduced: the only categories of finds that appeared throughout the life of the shrines and temples were coins and brooches, and brooches did not occur in large numbers. The first-century assemblage was dominated by ceramic jars and iron projectile heads, the latter possibly suggestive of a cult possessing martial aspects. In the later Roman period these categories were represented also, but only in the form of miniatures. The tiny clay vessels and the lead tablets were the most numerous find categories recovered from contexts dating to the middle and late Roman periods and all the miniature weapons from the final Roman phases were spears. This trend of miniaturization went hand in hand with two other processes – a tendency towards simplification and, secondly, a diversification of types. The complex full-size tools, weapons, lead tablets, spoons and toilet articles, and objects involving various different materials such as the brooches, were replaced through time by simpler items involving less elaborate methods of manufacture: miniature spears, sheet metal plaques, the flat copper alloy rings, simple finger rings, bracelets and glass beads. The process of diversification is mainly represented by the growing incidence of the offering of small items of jewellery during the fourth century. This was not due entirely to the more general increase in the occurrence of such flimsy trinkets, as we shall see when some other fourth-century assemblages are considered below. It can be concluded that the votive objects deposited at Uley become smaller, simpler and more numerous through time and that a distinctly martial aspect apparent in the first-century assemblage diminished to a great extent and faded within the more personal connections of the fourth-century offerings. These displayed remarkable concentrations of circular and ring-shaped objects: coins, flat copper alloy rings, bracelets and finger rings. The potential significance of these changes will be discussed further below in relation to an assessment of the cults indicated by the inscriptions, sculptures and figurines.

On a few sites it has been possible also to study the patterning of finds across space; that is the distribution of different categories in relation to the excavated structures, boundaries and courtyards. At Woodeaton finds were concentrated in the area of the *temenos* between the temple entrance and the main gateway of the enclosure while even more find-spots occurred in the zone just outside this gateway. This information has been used to suggest that booths and stalls may have been erected in these areas for the purpose of selling votive objects, and probably other commodities, to the pilgrims and to passing travellers. At Uley several distributions have been investigated: the pattern of votive finds, grouped by function and raw material, but not separated by chronological divisions, is shown in **57**. In spite of the widespread occurrence of the movement of votive objects subsequent to their initial deposition, the greatest concentration of votive objects was centred on the temple building

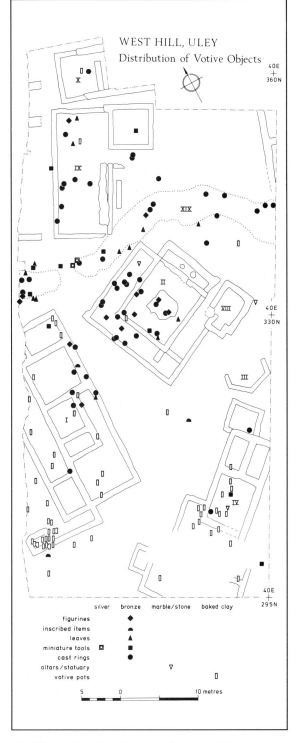

57 *Uley: the distribution of votive objects among the excavated buildings. Structure II is the Roman temple.*

itself, and most of the figurines and stone sculpture fragments were found within or very close to it. Occupation deposits in structure IX, north of the temple, contained mainly metal leaves and flat-cast rings. As some rings had casting flanges still attached, it can be inferred that production took place on site. This structure also contained some evidence for metal-working and may therefore have formed a manufacturing focus within the complex. The distributions of objects over buildings I and IV to the south represent the spreads of votive material deposited over the demolished remains of those structures in the late fourth century AD. The spreads of miniature pots in these locations may suggest an early- to mid-fourth-century date for this class of material. The distribution of fittings, mainly from boxes and furniture, was also concentrated in the temple itself while the pattern of deposition of jewellery was more widespread. The concentration of objects of antler, shale and jet in one of the rooms of ancillary building IV might indicate the site of a shop.

The symbolism of votive objects

In order to investigate the nature and ideological components of the finds assemblage more fully, the incidence of selected categories of material has been compared for a series of seven temple sites, mainly located in the west of England (**58**). The finds have been quantified from the published reports and the totals have been limited to drawn or described diagnostic items, and do not include unpublished fragments, except in the case of Lydney where the stated totals for copper alloy bracelets and bone or metal pins have been employed, even though only a small selection were illustrated or described in the report. It is clear from this that certain types of personal items and jewellery occurred in particularly large numbers in different temple assemblages. A similar peaking is detectable also amongst the categories of votive objects and fittings. Each temple assemblage appears to have been characterized by the incidence of sharp peaks in the numbers of one or more specific categories of object. The peaks are shown by denser shading on the chart and can be listed as follows:

Uley	votive copper alloy rings; miniature pots; finger rings
Lydney	bracelets; pins; spoons
Nettleton Scrubb	brooches; pins; spoons; finger rings
Henley Wood	brooches; pins; counters
Woodeaton	plaques; brooches; toilet articles; miniature tools or weapons
Harlow	brooches
Lamyatt Beacon	miniature tools or weapons

It could be argued in the case of the smaller assemblages, such as those from Henley Wood, Harlow and Lamyatt, that the surviving array of objects is not representative of the original assemblage of objects in use on the site. However, for the larger assemblages at least, the differences noted in the numerical composition do seem to be real, and they are of considerable importance to any discussion of cults represented. The incidence of brooches may be due to chronological rather than ideological factors, as they were in fashion mainly during the earlier Roman period, and thus will be more commonly found on temple sites that were frequented in the early centuries of Roman rule. This argument might apply particularly at Harlow and Nettleton. Otherwise it seems likely that the concentrations of particular object classes were related to the cult or cults practised at the individual temples. The prevalent finds categories seem to fall into three major groups – objects of martial aspect (weapons); different types of ring and disc, possibly including coins; and finally personal trinkets – bracelets, pins, spoons and toilet articles. These groups of objects can be linked to our knowledge of cults practised at the various temples, gleaned from inscriptions and representations of identifiable deities.

At Uley the evidence from stone sculpture, figurines and inscriptions demonstrates that the main deity worshipped was Mercury, along with his associates the goat and cockerel. The direct evidence for this included two statues, two altars (**59**), six figurines, six separate *caducei*, one depiction of the god on a sheet plaque and the name of Mercury inscribed on two copper alloy items and on at least 20 of the lead tablets. It has been suggested also that several other categories of finds could be associated with the cult of Mercury. In the light of Mercury's caring for trade and markets, the coins and all the rings may have been considered suitable offerings and, furthermore, the simple

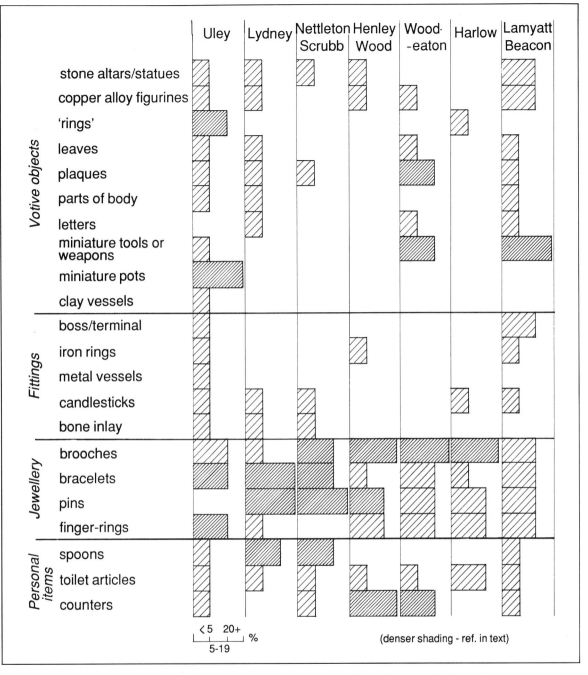

58 *The distribution of object types in seven temple assemblages.*

projections on some of the key rings (see **55**) may represent *caducei*. The incidence of votive legs and the plaque fragment bearing a foot may also be linked to the cult of Mercury, but in this case relating to his role as a god of travellers, who also was effective in the cure of diseases impeding movement. The supremacy of the cult of Mercury was confirmed by the animal bone evidence. Very high percentages of sheep/goat bones, with male goats generally in the majority, and large numbers of adult male domestic fowl bones relate very neatly to a cult which involved the veneration of the

75

goat and cockerel. The skulls and lower leg bones of the fowl were under-represented, suggesting that the birds were prepared away from the site, while butchery evidence indicated that goat horn cores were removed near the temple and that the carcases were probably eaten after sacrifice. A study of the ages of the animals at death showed that the main concentration of sacrifices lay in the autumn.

Other deities represented once only amongst the Uley finds included Sol and Jupiter, probably signifying days of the week, Cupid or Victory and a naked child, interpreted as Bacchus succoured by Mercury. However, one further deity was mentioned four times in the lead tablets. This was the god Mars, whose single name occurred twice on tablets, while inscriptions addressed to Mars Silvanus also occured twice, in both cases overwritten by the name of Mercury. The miniature spears could also be linked with the equestrian warrior cult of Mars. As we have seen, the miniature

spears may reflect the earlier deposition of full-size weapons in the votive deposits of the first century AD. Although sheep/goat bones were dominant in these early deposits, the goat was not prominent until around AD 100. It may therefore be that an existing warrior cult was gradually subsumed by the cult of Mercury as time progressed. Scholars have pointed out that the Celtic role of Mars in Gaul was partly similar to that of Mercury. Silvanus was a Roman nature-deity who was fairly commonly mentioned in Gaul and often associated with Sucellus, who was, like Mercury, a god of prosperity.

Evidence for a martial cult comes also from Lamyatt Beacon where the excavator has suggested that the survival of three depictions of Mars (two in stone and one a copper alloy figurine), the five horseman brooches (see **54**) and the array of model weapons: spears, axes and sickles, might signify that Mars was the supreme deity worshipped at the temple. He further noted that the antler deposits may indicate a conflation with a deity of Cernunnos type connected with hunting. Other deities represented by figurines at Lamyatt were Apollo (in stone), Jupiter, Mercury (twice) Minerva, Hercules and a Genius. At Nettleton, it has been suggested that the major cult figure was Apollo, who was represented on an inscribed bronze plaque and on an intaglio, and referred to as Apollo Cunomaglos ('Hound Lord') on a reused stone altar (**60**). Other deities represented once each were Silvanus and Diana, whilst four items could more or less certainly be taken as indicative of a subsidiary cult of Mercury: a relief of Mercury and his consort Rosmerta; a further relief possibly depicting Mercury; and two cockerels – one a terracotta head and the other a copper alloy candlestick.

The name of the god venerated at Lydney is known to have been Nodens. This Celtic name may refer to a god of hunting or fishing, and depictions of sea-monsters, fish and anchors on various bronzes, and a mosaic frieze, certainly suggest marine connections. The figures of dogs, six in stone and nine in copper alloy,

59 *Stone altar with a sculpture of Mercury flanked by a goat, or ram, and cockerel, from the temple at Uley. The figures had been defaced prior to reuse as a paving slab in a later building (quarter actual size).*

were linked by the excavator to a cult of healing, similar to those known from the classical world. (In classical Greece sacred dogs were kept at healing centres to lick limbs, or other affected body parts of the sick.) The occurrence of a dog's head above the inscription on a votive tablet addressed to Nodens further indicated that he may have possessed a healing aspect. The large numbers of pins and bracelets were envisaged as offerings in connection with the healing cult and equivalent to those given at Greek temples by women at the time of childbirth. The cult of Nodens therefore appears to have combined a simple nature cult, possibly with an element of hunting or fishing, with a major healing cult served by the guesthouse, specialist bath house and long building.

No clear indication of specific cults has been recovered at Harlow, Woodeaton or Henley Wood. At Woodeaton there were depictions of Venus, a Celtic goddess, Minerva, Cupid and possibly Hercules, and three representations of Mars. The miniature weapons and tools could be related to the worship of Mars, but the seven bronze eagles would more properly be associated with Jupiter. In addition, the presence of bronze snakes, a possible childbirth charm, and feminine toilet articles and miniature bracelets, would suggest the existence of a cult of healing. No depictions of known deities have been found at Harlow or Henley Wood, but the figurine of a Celtic goddess from the latter site has been linked with the finding of many personal items, especially brooches and counters, and animal bone deposits, to suggest the former presence of a cult possibly connected with fertility and fecundity.

The three groups of small votives isolated above, namely miniature weapons and tools, personal trinkets and the coincidence of rings, discs and money, can be seen to represent three major cult forms present in the Romano-Celtic religion of Britain. The miniature weapons denote a martial cult, the personal trinkets are indicative of cults devoted to the realms of fecundity and healing, whilst the incidence of large numbers of coins, rings and discs is seen

to be typical of the cult of Mercury. The Mercury cult is best exemplified at Uley, where additional evidence from the faunal remains has confirmed the primary dedication beyond doubt. A subsidiary cult of Mars has been identified also; this may have been more prevalent prior to the second century AD and related more closely to the preceding Celtic cult practised on the site. Other temples probably dedicated to Mars were Lamyatt and Woodeaton, although at Woodeaton there were strong indications also of a secondary cult or aspect. These indications were depictions of Venus, a female fertility goddess in the Celtic world, and her son Cupid, along with considerable quantities of toilet articles and miniature bracelets. These objects suggest a cult concerned with feminine fecundity, rather than a generalized healing aspect. A similar cult has been suggested for

60 *Stone altar from Nettleton Scrubb, bearing an inscription dedicating it to Apollo Cunomaglos. The epithet Cunomaglos (Hound Prince) may indicate that the god was worshipped here in his guise of archer or healer.*

Henley Wood on the basis of an unidentified, but definitely female, figurine, and the occurrence of many personal trinkets as well as food deposits.

The great healing complex at Lydney was dedicated to Nodens, possibly a god of hunting and fishing, and as noted above the healing aspect of the cult was evidenced by the representations of dogs and the many hundreds of pins and bracelets. Apparently spoons were also connected with the rituals enacted there. The octagonal temple at Nettleton was also dedicated to a hunter, but in the more classical form of Apollo, the archer. The epithet Cunomaglos, applied to Apollo on the stone altar, may indicate that the great god was worshipped there in his guise of archer and healer. The large numbers of pins and spoons may reflect a healing aspect, as at Lydney. On the other hand, the high occurrence of finger rings at Nettleton might suggest that Mercury was being venerated also, as at Uley, and indeed we find at Nettleton that Mercury himself was represented twice on stone reliefs and by two depictions of cockerels.

So far we have concentrated on offerings that were made from long-lasting substances such as metal, stone, antler or baked clay, which are also, therefore, the items that have survived the passage of time. However, we know from the literary sources that, at least in the Roman period, most offerings and sacrifices were of an organic nature: foodstuffs such as fruits or cereals, juices and beverages containing alcohol, or the flesh of animals. For pre-Roman times there are also strong hints that human sacrifice was also practised. In the Iron Age we have seen that groves or individual trees could be sacred and that carved timber figures or tree-trunk totem poles were employed as components in some of the shrines. Elements of trees also seem to have been used as votive offerings. None of these survive from shrines at ground level, but examples of whole trees, logs and branches thrown into ritual shafts are well known from this period on the continent of Europe. Such a practice appears to have continued into the Roman period in Britain, where deposits of tree-trunks, logs, twigs or nuts occurred in 16 per cent of 102 shafts for which details have been recorded. The species represented most commonly were oak, hazel and birch. The only recently excavated waterlogged temple deposit, the sacred spring at Bath, predictably produced samples of twigs and nuts.

Sacrifice

The Celts were fascinated by animals and the sacrifice of living beasts formed a major part of their religious activities. Animal bones recovered from some of the shrines have shown that particular species were preferred in different areas, although they were always domestic animals. At Harlow and Hayling Island, sheep and lambs were best represented in the Iron Age deposits, while at Uley there was an articulated limb of a cow. The South Cadbury shrine burials included at least 16 cattle, 3 pigs, 3 sheep and horse, many of them juveniles. More widespread was the deliberate deposition of complete animal skeletons, skulls, mandibles or articulated limbs in the base of worn-out storage pits on settlement sites and hillforts. These remains were found in pits amongst the residential structures and may be interpreted as the result of animal sacrifices that were carried out in a domestic context, perhaps by family leaders rather than by religious specialists. Cattle were by far the most frequently represented, although horse and dog were also common candidates. Sheep were noticeably under-represented and pig deposits were confined almost entirely to the hillforts. Pork is the meat of warrior champions, who may have been based in the hillforts, and dog and horse often functioned as symbols for particular deities. The horse was associated with Epona, and dogs with Nantosuelta or the Apollo Cunomaglos, 'Hound Lord', evidenced at Nettleton. No doubt the sacrificing of animals would have occurred alongside the donation of vegetable foods, libations of alcoholic liquids and other items. It can be assumed that many of the sacrificed beasts would have provided meat for feasting, so the numbers of bodies and parts of bodies that have survived on Iron Age sites indicate that the practice of animal sacrifice in Celtic society must have been very widespread indeed.

The sacrificial habit continued unabated in Romano-British society. Connections between men and deities were achieved through the means of prayer and sacrifice. The prayers needed to be word-perfect, repeated for the prescribed number of times and declaimed in a suitable tone and manner. Furthermore, the Roman gods were more likely to respond to requests if a donation accompanied the prayer. This donation could take the form of a sacrifice of food or the offering of a valuable object: a blood sacrifice was often obligatory. The animal victim may have been decorated with garlands of flowers and would have been ritually prepared by a priest, with music playing to drown any sounds of ill-omen, all accompanied by the burning of incense. Then the beast would have been pole-axed by another specialist, the throat cut and the liver expertly removed. The liver became the subject of inspection by the 'gut-gazers' (*haruspices*), who could interpret the signs of divine direction from the convolutions of the gory organ. Subsequently, the ritual feast could begin. In the Roman period animal sacrifices were effective only if undertaken by an official priest and his assistants. Thus it is to the temple sites that we should look for evidence of the practice in Britain. Ox skulls were found below the floors of temple buildings at Muntham Court (Sussex) and St Albans (the Triangular Temple) and also at Chanctonbury (Sussex). There were pig and bird burials at Hockwold and we may recall the ritual burials of birds found in the well at Jordan Hill, Dorset. At Brigstock (Northants.) there was a sheep burial and sheep were also the most common species amongst the more numerous remains from the temples at Hayling Island, Haddenham (Cambridgeshire) and Harlow. On the last site 80 per cent of animal bones from stratified deposits were of sheep or goat. Detailed analysis showed that the majority were in fact sheep and that most had been killed when they were still lambs. An even higher percentage of sheep/goat bones were recorded at Uley, but in this case most of the animals were goats. As noted above, the overall preponderance of sheep and goats, and the presence of domestic fowl, could easily be explained in the context of a cult involving the worship of Mercury and his associates, the goat, ram and cockerel. Mature male goats seem to have been preferred and the deliberate removal of frontals and horn cores apparently formed a characteristic of the cult.

The evidence for human sacrifice at shrines in Iron Age Britain is slight, although, as in the case of the evidence of animals considered above, many skeletons or fragments of bodies have been found in pits and ditches on settlement sites and hillforts. Unlike the animal remains in settlements, however, the human remains are thought to reflect the burial of criminals or other outcasts from society rather than the victims of sacrificial rites. A possible exception to this is the series of complete male skeletons which have been discovered beneath hillfort ramparts, and which may be the result of sacrificial foundation burial. The only evidence from the shrines themselves are infant foundation burials from Uley and Maiden Castle, plus the adult thigh bone and a single molar tooth from the Uley ditch. In Europe evidence for human sacrifice is more persuasive and we may note with interest the recent discovery of a huge heap of hundreds of human limb bones, most probably the remains of sacrifices, below the Roman sanctuary of Ribemont-sur-Ancre in Picardy, France. The human remains derived from 200 to 250 young men and, at the nearby sanctuary of Gournay, the remains of bodies which had been beheaded with axes have been identified.

Much of our understanding of human sacrifice in the Celtic realms depends on interpretation of passages in classical texts. The texts concerned were mainly written in the first or second centuries AD, but were in part merely repeating an earlier ethnography of the Celts written by Posidonius, a Greek historian of the late second century BC. The main problem with these texts is that they were written for political or other Romano-centric reasons and cannot necessarily be taken at face value. In particular the Roman authors tended to overemphasize the horrific nature of the sacrificial behaviour of the Celts in Gaul and beyond, behaviour which was perceived to be completely at odds with the 'civilized' practices of the Mediterranean world. Bearing these points in mind, some of the more relevant passages may be summarized. Strabo records that human victims were sometimes killed by arrows or impaled inside their temples. The same author, as well as Julius Caesar, describes the extraordinary giant figures fabricated from wickerwork. These were filled with human and animal victims who were subsequently burnt alive in a horrifying sacrificial conflagration. Tacitus described the Druids in Britain who 'deemed it indeed a duty to cover their altars with the blood of captives and to consult their deities through human entrails'. This process of divination was also highlighted by Diodorus Siculus, although in the case he describes it is achieved through a study of the death-throes of the victim:

They have also certain philosophers and theologians who are treated with special honour, whom they call Druids. They further make use of seers, thinking them worthy of high praise. These latter by their augural observances and by the sacrifice of sacrificial animals can foretell the future and they hold all the people subject to them. In particular when enquiring into matters of great import they have a strange and incredible custom; they devote to death a human being and stab him with a dagger in the region above the diaphragm, and when he has fallen they foretell the future from his fall, and from the convulsions of his limbs and, moreover, from the spurting of the blood, placing their trust in some ancient and long-continued observation of these practices.

Human sacrifice was not allowed within the Roman empire and there is no concrete evidence for the practice even in such a far-flung province as Britain. At Springhead in Kent there were four infant burials, two of them decapitated, below the corners of temple IV, but these babies may have died naturally and were not necessarily the result of sacrificial rites. We may note also the finding of human skull fragments from the Roman levels at Hayling Island and a scatter of teeth and pieces of skull from the demolition layers at Uley. In both cases though, these items may derive from burials from the unexcavated surrounding areas which have been ploughed for many decades. More convincing in a ritual context are the skulls preserved in oil from the site of the basilica at Wroxeter (Shropshire). Possibly the carefully preserved relics of sacrificial victims or trophies of war, these items may have been kept within the Roman basilica. Alternatively they may have belonged to an overlying shrine of the final or post-Roman era. As will be seen below there was a dramatic revival of interest in disembodied skulls and other body fragments during the early Christian period, although it took place in a totally different ideological environment.

1 The ruins of the medieval church of Knowlton, located within a surviving henge monument of late Neolithic origin.

2 Detached head from a larger than life cult statue of Mercury, found during excavation of the Roman temple at Uley.

3 Artist's reconstruction of the interior of the Roman temple at Uley.

4 Miniature silver spearhead from Uley. The blade is pierced for suspension and the twisted stem has been ritually bent or 'killed'.

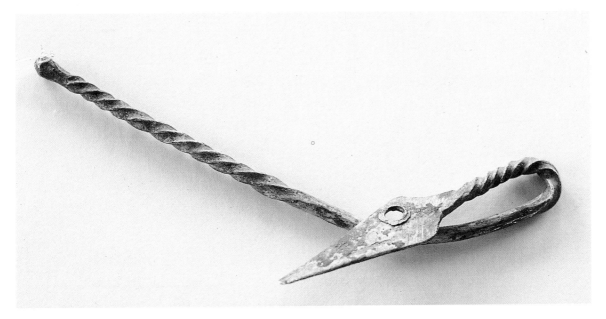

5 Plait of red hair from a late Roman plaster burial at Crown Buildings, Dorchester.

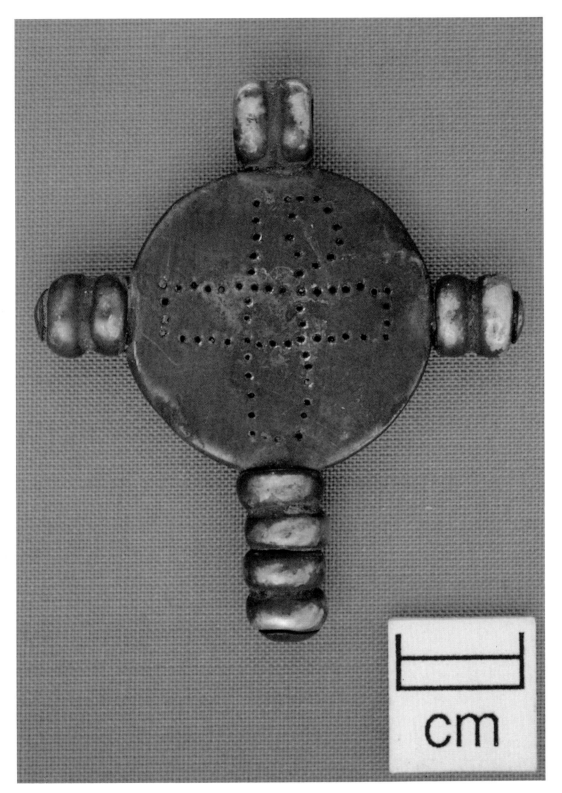

6 Silver pendant found in a late Roman grave at Shepton Mallet. Three ornamental arms and a suspension loop surround a reused Roman coin, which bears a roughly executed chi-rho symbol outlined by small circular punch marks.

8 *(Above)* Central roundel of the mosaic from the Hinton St Mary villa. The figure, thought to be a portrait of Christ, overlies a chi-rho symbol and is flanked by pomegranates, symbols of the Life Eternal.

7 *(Left)* Copper alloy mounting from a casket, found tightly folded in the temple debris at Uley. The repoussé decoration depicts four biblical scenes.

9 The holy waters of St Winifred's Well at Holywell, viewed through the towering arches of the medieval cover building.

10 The hoard of silver objects from Water Newton: bowls, jugs, cups, dish, strainer and leaf-shaped plaques. Several items bear inscribed chi-rho symbols and the items may have functioned as church plate used by early Christians.

6

Burials and cemeteries

Whilst to many members of modern society disposal of dead human bodies is regarded as the clinical removal of matter from the domestic environment, to our forbears the rites of burial for their companions were deeply enmeshed in strongly held religious beliefs. Most often these included belief in an afterlife, enacted in a supernatural world governed by one or more deities. Burial of a dead body was viewed as the first step in transference to this other world and to reunification with the all-important ancestors. In Britain the rite of individual burial, either by inhumation or cremation, beneath a round barrow was common in the Early Bronze Age and the rich accoutrements of some of the graves in the Wessex heartland are some of the best-known objects from the prehistoric period in England. By the Middle Bronze Age, cremation was the standard rite and groups of burials, sometimes contained in pottery vessels and occasionally accompanied by small objects, such as a metal finger ring or a bead, were interred in groups. These groups were placed near to small farms or settlement sites and contained numbers of males and females and various age groups, thus suggesting that family groups of a few generations were represented. However, by the Late Bronze Age period evidence for such burial behaviour had disappeared and, apart from a series of skulls tossed into major rivers, no human bones can be dated to this period.

It used to be thought that the same situation pertained within the earlier Iron Age, and such was the profound impact of the apparent lack of burials for the Early Iron Age that scholars were inspired to use the absence of a burial rite as a defining negative characteristic for the Early Iron Age 'Woodbury Culture'. However, the discoveries during a series of major excavation campaigns on Iron Age hillforts and settlements during the last 20 years, and several programmes of detailed research, have revolutionized our understanding of Iron Age mortuary rituals. A wide variety of burial modes can be recognized and interpreted in relation to our knowledge of Iron Age religious beliefs. The more formal and regular rites date from the later stages of the Iron Age and three specific regional groups practising single burial have been recognized, each defined by a particular array of grave features and associated rites and objects, as well as a more widespread, but rarer, incidence of bodies buried with swords (see p. 83). In contrast to these were the Late Iron Age cremation cemeteries of south-eastern England with their characteristic cinerary urns and distinctly continental aspect.

Earlier Iron Age burials

For the earlier periods of the Iron Age, new studies have been based largely on the results from a series of major excavations, mainly in the south of England, which have produced large numbers of human remains. The sites concerned include settlements such as Gussage All Saints (Dorset) and Winnall Down (Hants.), along with the major hillforts of Hod Hill (Dorset), Winklebury and Danebury (both in Hants.). In order to give an impression of the scale of increased evidence now available it is necessary only to point out that Winnall Down produced remains from 204 human individuals, whilst from the first ten years of excavation at Danebury 59 particular burials can be isolated from the bones representing a minimum of 70 people. Most of these burials were deposited in disused grain storage pits.

Analysis of all these remains has led to the recent definition of a series of different types of inhumation burial (cremation was not a preferred rite in the earlier Iron Age), according to the degree of completeness of the skeleton. For it appears that many burials contained only parts of a body, especially bodies without heads, heads without bodies, and bodies with one or more limbs removed. To this apparently gruesome picture may be added the special burial of selected individual bones, which in some cases may represent the 'missing links' from partial burials interred elsewhere.

In the Early Iron Age, complete skeletons occurred rarely and only in hillforts, but by the Middle and Late Bronze Age they were more common and were found also on settlement sites. In particular they occurred underneath hillfort ramparts, and these burials may be interpreted as foundation deposits, or sacrifices. Skeletons with pieces missing, and the interments of single articulated arms or legs, were found almost entirely in hillforts and date mainly from the Early or the Late Iron Age. It may be that these are the remains of 'massacre' victims or the result of epidemic disease. Certainly they date from two periods of particular social stress that may have induced phases of chronic warfare (around 400 and 100 BC respectively). They might also have been victims of human sacrifice – or cannibalism – but few traces of butchery marks on the bones have been recognized. One particularly puzzling feature is that partial skeletons buried on their own tend to be of females while multiple partial burials are more likely to be male. Incidence of the burial of single skulls are mostly male and generally have been found at the bottom of pits inside hillforts. Some of these may have been trophies gained in martial head-hunting, or have derived from rituals connected with the more general Celtic cult of the human head (see p. 54).

The final category of burial deposits is in many ways the most interesting. On settlement sites dating to the Early Iron Age, and throughout the Iron Age at hillforts, the interment of

individual human bones, as opposed to articulated limbs or incomplete skeletons, was quite common. The types of bones represented are usually skull fragments and long bones and, where detailed analysis has been possible, it has been ascertained that more single bones derive from the right side of the body than from the left. This evidence seems to suggest that corpses were manipulated, probably after the initial process of decay, and that carefully selected bones may have been stored, hidden or used for ritual purposes on occupation sites prior to their individual burial at a later date.

Studies of the detailed findspots of burials within individual sites has led to the further conclusion that burials were not interred at random but occurred in clusters at chosen

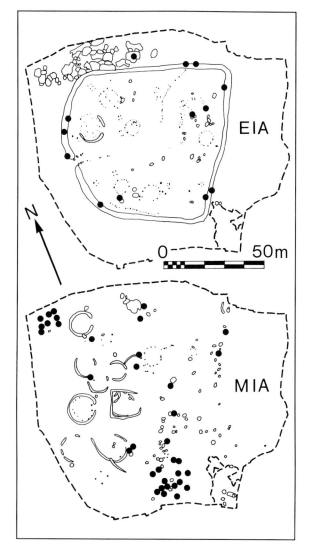

61 *The distribution of human remains, denoted by black dots, in two phases of Iron Age settlement at Winnall Down.*

locations within or outside zones of occupation. In some cases burials were made in close proximity to settlement areas, notably at Hod Hill, in one group of burials at Winklebury, and at Danebury, where a very complex picture is emerging. At Hod Hill the burials clustered in and around two 'horseshoe' shaped enclosure ditches which may have been ritual structures. More commonly, however, burials were concentrated away from the settled areas and were located in the fillings of enclosure ditches, or in groups of pits at some distance from the houses. This situation occurred at Winklebury, at Gussage All Saints and at Winnall Down (61). On this site, in the Early Iron Age (EIA), burials consisting mainly of single bones had been placed away from the houses, especially in the enclosure ditch, while in the Middle Iron Age (MIA) phase of occupation burials, now of the partial or complete skeleton type, were interred in two main areas – south-east of the house sites and in a discrete area just to the north-west.

Although finds such as these have provoked a totally new approach to Iron Age funerary customs, it must be stressed that only a minority of the population are represented by these rites. Thus at Danebury it has been estimated that the bodies recovered derive from only 6 per cent of the population and that remains of 90 to 95 per cent of the people who occupied the hillfort have disappeared without trace. It seems that the invisible burial rite current in the Late Bronze Age therefore must have continued as the norm for most of the Iron Age population.

Late Iron Age cemeteries
In comparison with these enigmatic complexities, the characteristics of the later Iron Age regional groups of specific inhumation types may be summarized with ease. Known since the antiquarian diggings of Greenwell and Mortimer, the burials of men and women on the Yorkshire Wolds contained in graves below barrows with square ditches were long the best-known example of an Iron Age inhumation tradition in Britain. The square-plan barrows occur in extensive cemetery groups or small family clusters, and certain high-ranking individuals were accompanied by the remains of wheeled vehicles – the so-called chariot burials – and occasionally by small ornaments such as copper alloy brooches or bracelets, and

horse fittings. Although links with people who employed a similar burial rite in the Marne region of France are attested, some features of the Yorkshire tradition, such as the crouched attitude of the body, are firmly rooted in native practice.

Crouched burials are also found in the south-west of England, although in this case they are commonly contained within cist-graves lined and covered with slabs or boulders of the local slate and granite. These graves occur in small cemeteries around the coast of Cornwall and on the Isles of Scilly and, as in Yorkshire, a few individuals were accompanied by small ornaments of metal, in this case brooches, pins and rings, or exotic items such as shale bracelets and glass beads.

Richer than the accompanied graves of either Yorkshire or the south-west are the widely distributed but rare examples of skeletons buried with a sword, and sometimes pieces of associated weaponry or regalia such as shields or sword suspension rings. Some of these bodies are crouched and may represent exceptionally high-ranking warriors within the native populations, although the incidence of some extended burials with swords raises the possibility that they may reflect the influence of continental settlers arriving just after the Roman conquest.

A third regional group of inhumation burials is known from south Dorset where a section of the tribe known as the Durotriges began in the first century BC to bury their dead crouched, usually lying on the right side, within simple earth-dug graves located in small discrete cemeteries (62). Compared with the other inhuming groups, the provision of grave goods is more widespread and they include pottery vessels, metal ornaments such as brooches, occasional weapons and, quite commonly, the remains of a joint of meat. The known cemeteries, of which the 'War Cemetery' at Maiden Castle is the most famous, have been augmented by the meticulous excavation of 67 burials, divisible into three groups, at Poundbury (63). The relative occurrence of males, females and children is shown in the histograms – there were most males in the 'War Cemetery' and most children in the Poundbury group, which may have included some foundation burials associated with contemporary buildings. The central histograms show the clear preference for the crouched attitude, with body lying on

62 *Durotrigian crouched burial from Poundbury: a complete pot lies between the arms.*

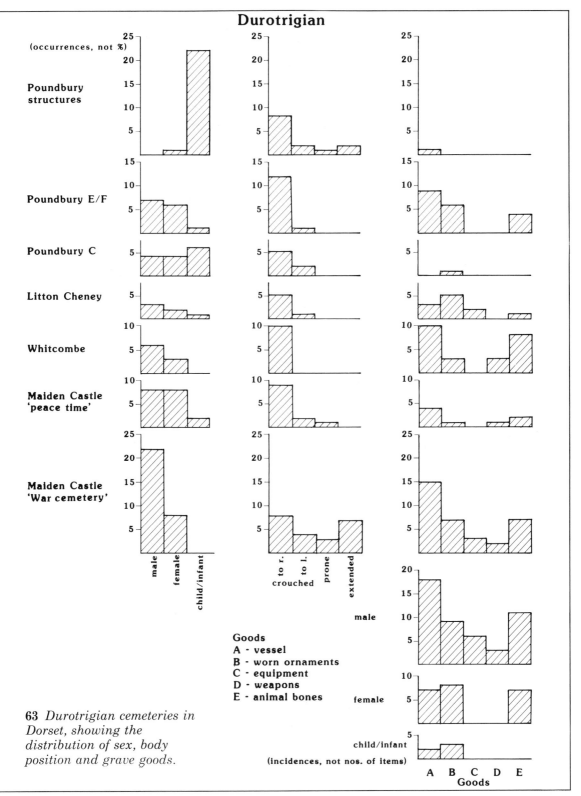

Durotrigian

(occurrences, not %)

Poundbury structures

Poundbury E/F

Poundbury C

Litton Cheney

Whitcombe

Maiden Castle 'peace time'

Maiden Castle 'War cemetery'

male   female   child/infant

to r.   to l.   prone   extended
crouched

male

female

child/infant

(incidences, not nos. of items)

A B C D E
Goods

Goods
A - vessel
B - worn ornaments
C - equipment
D - weapons
E - animal bones

63 *Durotrigian cemeteries in Dorset, showing the distribution of sex, body position and grave goods.*

the right, amongst all the known cemeteries, whilst the third set of diagrams shows the incidence of different types of grave goods. Vessels, ornaments and animal bone deposits are most commonly found, with the rarer items of weapons and equipment being confined to male burials only. In most of the cemeteries males were more often provided with goods than females, and in general the burials of children were not furnished, suggesting that wealth or status came with advancing age.

In total contrast with all the rites discussed so far are the cremations of the so-called 'Aylesford Culture' of south-east England. These were contained in pottery vessels and subsequently interred in flat graves within small cemetery areas. The pottery containers are similar to those used in France and the rite was prevalent from about 50 BC up to the Roman conquest and beyond, when the cremation rite becomes that commonly employed by the early Roman population of Britain. A few graves of outstanding richness have been discovered, containing objects linked mainly with both feasting – pottery platters and iron fire dogs; and drinking – amphorae, strainers and drinking vessels of pottery, glass and silver.

Outside the areas of the regional inhumation groups and the zone of the Aylesford cremation cemeteries, we have seen that the newly-defined burial modes of complete, partial or fragmentary inhumation in pits and ditches were confined to a relatively small percentage of the population. The lack of any grave goods, and the absence of provision of any prestige indicator such as a barrow mound, suggest that these graves were unlikely to have been those of a political or social elite. Some may represent the victims of sacrifice but the most likely explanation is that they contain the remains of society's outcasts – criminals or religious heretics, suicides, those killed by drowning, travellers away from home or mothers who died in childbirth. The only possible exception to this are the single bones which may be the venerated relics of particularly special individuals. The majority of the population received a burial rite which is invisible to the archaeologist: long-term exposure of the body, or cremation followed by scattering of the ashes on land or water. Such rites certainly would have been in accord with the spiritual world view of the Celts, centred as it was on the powers of nature and the elements.

Roman burial rites

By the early Roman period the situation had changed dramatically and, following the main features of the Aylesford cremation cemeteries, a burial rite of cremation for all spread rapidly through the province. Many burials were provided with goods which were intended to afford a feast for the dead – food bones, vessels and cups – sometimes augmented by substances to provide a sweet-smelling atmosphere (herbs, flowers or perfumes), or a light-giving lamp. A general impression of mundane repetition pervades, but, as the centuries progressed, strong belief in the after-life developed, and associated with this, a growth in the incidence of inhumation may be documented. Thus, by the late Roman period there were many large cemeteries full of skeletons and grave goods, and these have provided ideal sets of evidence for the archaeologist to analyse. Late Roman cemeteries do not generally contain very large numbers of richly furnished graves and consequently did not undergo the degree of antiquarian investigation, and unwitting destruction, that was lavished upon their Anglo-Saxon counterparts. On the other hand, many archaeologists, and certainly the sources of finance, were unwilling to expend the effort required to excavate any of these vast cemeteries. However, by the 1960s a new generation of field archaeologists, keen to sample the potential of such sites, excavated a series of these cemeteries and recorded them to a very high standard indeed. It is the harvest of these extensive campaigns that is now beginning to be reaped. A selection of the more important sites are listed in (64), from which the considerable increase in data available for study may be appreciated.

Four Roman cemeteries

The general nature of these great late Roman cemeteries may be summarized by describing the main characteristics of four examples, three of these outside Roman towns, at Winchester (Lankhills), Ilchester and Dorchester (Poundbury) and the fourth, Cannington, next to a very long-lived hillfort. The site at Lankhills forms part of the northern extramural cemetery of Roman Winchester. Within the area excavated the graves appeared highly ordered with the burials aligned on local topographical features such as the Roman road and a major ditch (65; F12). The analysis of coin-dated graves

Site	County	Number of burials excavated	Decade of excavation
Ilchester	Somerset	61	70s
Lynch Farm	Northants.	50	70s
Alington Avenue	Dorset	73	80s
Lankhills	Hants.	451	60s–70s
Cirencester	Glos.	453	70s
Bradley Hill	Somerset	55	70s
Henley Wood	Avon	72	60s
Cannington	Somerset	542	60s
Ulwell	Dorset	54	80s
Poundbury	Dorset	c.1450	60s–70s

suggests that the cemetery had grown from west to east throughout the fourth century AD and had gradually expanded over the ditch (F12). East of this ditch most graves were for males and it seems that after about AD 350 female burials were confined mainly to the area to the west of it (see **65**). The graves were arranged in fairly neat rows, especially near to the ditch, although elsewhere end-to-end lines are more apparent. Few graves intercut each other and all were arranged with heads aligned approximately to the west. No obvious groupings of graves were present and no clusters of particular types or combinations of grave goods could be seen. However, a series of possible rich graves was defined on the basis of three criteria: graves with step construction; graves containing objects manufactured from exotic raw materials (glass, pewter, ivory or silver); and graves enclosed by a gully (see **65**). Such graves were found throughout the excavated area but tended to cluster in the southern area of the ditch (F12) and between and around gullies F2 and F6. Four of these gully enclosures had been constructed around single graves. The gullies may have been bedding trenches for hedges which enclosed the graves with rich goods. The grave associated with enclosure F6 included the remains of men, women and children. The elaboration of the graves suggested the burial of members of a wealthy or important family who were not subject to the normal rules of the cemetery. Five of the graves were furnished, and one contained a platter embellished with two possibly Christian symbols (see **73**).

The burials excavated west of Ilchester do not belong to a typical town cemetery but are more similar to those known from rural contexts. The Ilchester burials lie in end-to-end rows along the borders of property boundaries

64 *The scale of excavation at ten cemeteries of Roman and/or post-Roman date.*

running back from suburban properties which were probably agrarian in function. The excavated graves belonged to the fourth century AD and occurred in groups of 14, 28 and 15 burials. These may represent parts of the burial grounds for the members of individual households. No structures were associated with the graves and no burials were contained within stone or lead coffins. Indeed, the most remarkable grave was one containing a man and his dog. The graves often contained hobnailed boots and occasional iron knives; food bones or items of jewellery were also found. All this is in marked contrast to the little we know of the largely unexcavated cemetery lying to the east of Ilchester. Here at Northover there are neat rows of unfurnished graves in wooden coffins, interspersed with occasional coffins of stone or lead (**66**) and traces of stone-built cemetery structures. However, the western cemeteries can be paralleled at several recently excavated rural sites such as Lynch Farm (Northants.), where burials clustered in the corner of a paddock, and Bradley Hill (Somerset) where 57 simple burials in wooden coffins or slab-lined graves were located next to a Roman farm. In all these cases, goods were few, with hobnailed boots predominant.

The Roman town of Dorchester in Dorset is almost surrounded by cemeteries. Most of these contain burials of both rites, inhumation and cremation, associated with varying types and quantities of grave goods dating from the first to the fourth centuries AD. The graves are aligned in various directions. However, just north-west of the town defences there is a series of rather different burial grounds. These comprise neat rows of inhumation burials,

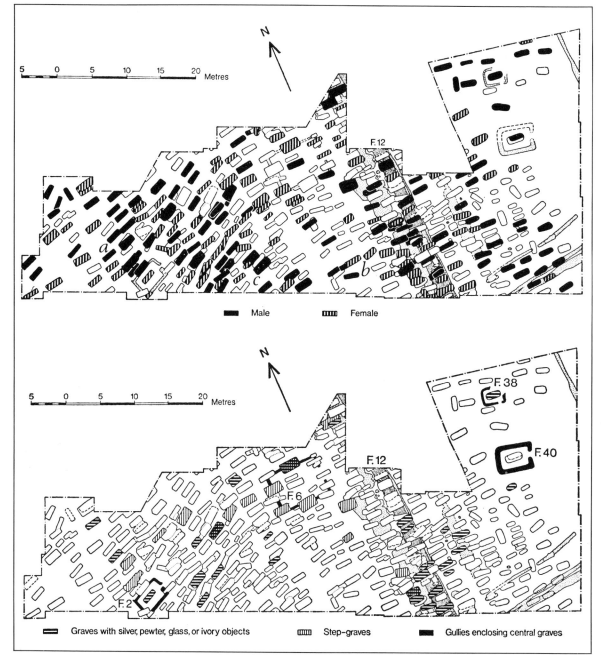

65 *Lankhills: (a) the distribution of male and female graves; (b) the distribution of special graves and graves containing exotic objects.*

mainly coffined but lacking in grave goods, and all with the head laid to the west. One of these cemeteries, lying just east of the ramparts of the Iron Age fort of Poundbury, has been excavated over many years, and a total of c.1450

burials has so far been recorded. Rows of large graves running in lines along the field boundaries behind a Roman farmstead were probably initiated in the second century AD (**67** and **68**). These contained a fair number of grave goods and hobnails, and were very similar to the burials beyond the western suburb of Ilchester described above.

Contemporary with at least some of these

graves, and continuing probably into the early fifth century AD, were the rows and rows of uniform west-east graves of the so-called 'main cemetery'. These were neatly arranged with the minimum of overlapping and probably had been marked by stones or posts. Grave goods were very few but some of the bodies had been laid to rest in substantial coffins of lead or stone. Within some of these coffins the dead body had been partially preserved by a packing of gypsum plaster; some pieces of clothing and even heads of hair had thus survived for archaeologists to analyse (**colour plate 5**). This evidence suggested that some of the burials had been treated as more special than others and, furthermore, some of these special burials had been singled out for burial within enclosures, as at Lankhills. At Poundbury such enclosures were of two forms: firstly some four-sided ditched enclosures lying on the south-west margin of the cemetery; but more significantly, some small stone-walled rectangular buildings interspersed within the grave rows in the body of the main cemetery (see **67**). These may have been roofed structures – certainly some of them were adorned inside with some highly decorative wall plaster – but the buildings may have been partly open to the elements, and some of the structures could have been simple gated enclosures defined only by low walls. They may have functioned as mausolea or as small chapels (or *memoriae*) over the burials of individuals who were the subject of particular veneration. The buildings contained small numbers of burials, ranging from two to seven, and included males and females, adults, juveniles and children. Whether these groups, or any other clusters of graves within the cemetery, represent the members of a single family unfortunately cannot be assessed on the biological evidence available.

The cemetery at Cannington lay on a hill close to an Iron Age hillfort; the latter may have been reoccupied in the late Roman or early post-Roman period. Excavation recovered 542 bodies from 400 graves, but it is estimated that a further 1000 or more graves had been destroyed by stone quarrying. The major series of radiocarbon dates for burials in the cemetery has shown that the burial ground was founded in the late Roman period and continued in use until the seventh or early eighth century AD. The layout of the burials indicates that there may have been a series of focal points around which graves were arranged, with heads generally aligned to the west (**69**). Within the central area rows of burials are evident, especially in the western and south-western sectors, and in the denser areas, many graves overlapped. To the west and to the east discrete groups of less closely spaced graves are found. Four excavated structures lay within or on the margins of the cemetery area that survived for archaeological investigation. These included three post-hole structures: one within the cemetery area (Structure I) may have been a church or chapel; another flanking a pathway approaching the cemetery from the north (Structure II) which may have functioned as a gatehouse or a further religious building; and a third, Structure III, in an area sparsely occupied by graves, which produced evidence for iron-working. To the north lay the circular 'Summit Structure' which was late Roman in date and could have been a shrine or temple with graves, or a mausoleum. Structure I, the

66 *Lead and stone coffins at Northover.*

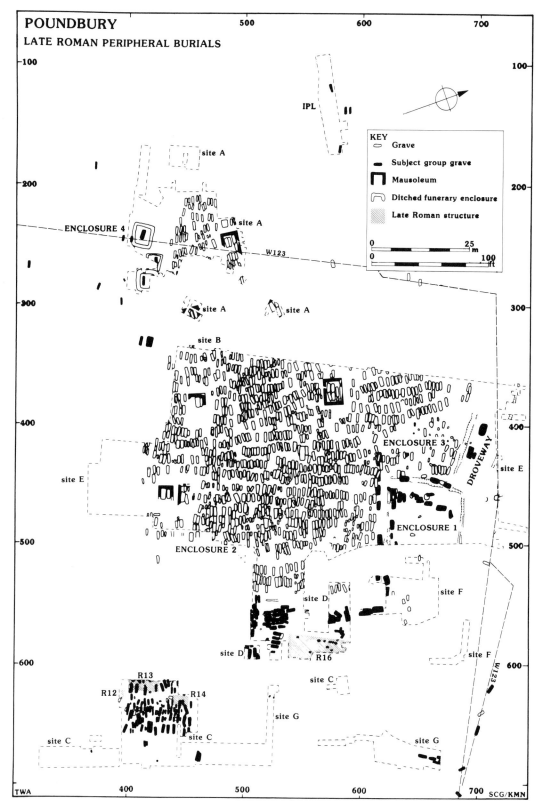

possible chapel, appears to have formed one focus for rows of graves which lie in a triangular arrangement to the east of it, whilst a second, and possibly later, focus was formed by a grave of a juvenile. This was marked with a cist-like structure formed of slabs of Lias limestone set in a mound over the grave; an associated marker of red sandstone was decorated with schematic signs or symbols. Grave goods were generally few in number and were dominated by items of domestic or personal equipment: a few Roman coins, some pins, beads, one comb and a series of knives, mainly of post-Roman type. Two infant graves of the seventh century included some interesting and unusual jewellery.

67 *Plan of the late Roman cemetery at Poundbury. The graves shaded in black were aligned on land boundaries and contained some grave goods. The rest, arranged in rows, were generally findless.*

68 *General view of late Roman graves at Poundbury.*

Most late Roman cemeteries contain the burials of men, women and children and it seems likely that all members of the population were buried in a similar location, possibly in family or community groups. Some cemeteries contained more males (Ilchester, Lynch Farm, Lankhills: east zone and Cirencester) but this is really only very marked at Cirencester where the burial of veterans may have been more common. While many children were buried at Lankhills: east zone, and Cirencester) but this children were under-represented. This was the case at Ilchester and at Lynch Farm. One interesting point concerning the distribution of age groups is that adults and infants or children are commonly found, but juveniles are less well represented. The reason for this general tendency is not yet clear, but the immigration of adults is one possible explanation.

Pagans and Christians

In the majority of late Roman and post-Roman cemeteries, the predominant burial rite involved the laying out of the body straight on

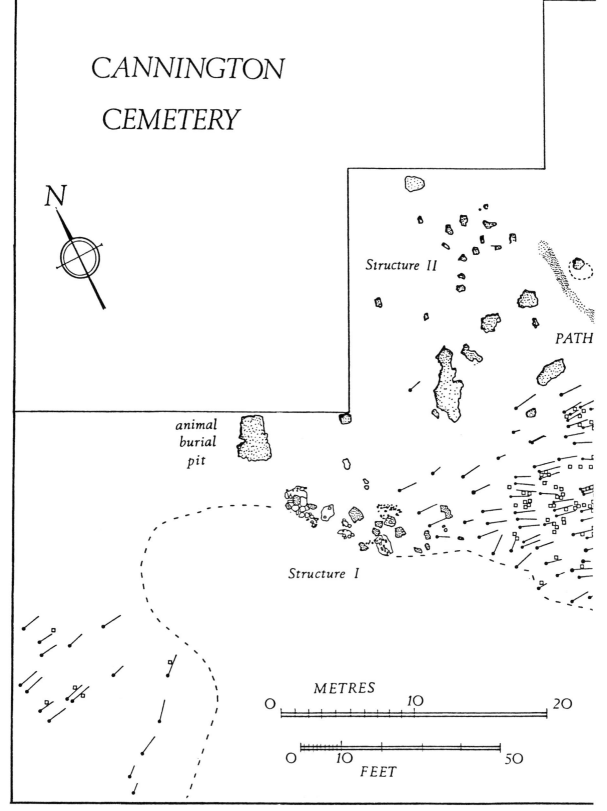

CANNINGTON
CEMETERY

N

Structure II

PATH

animal
burial
pit

Structure I

METRES
O   10   20

O   10   50
FEET

69 *Plan of the cemetery
and associated
structures at Cannington.*

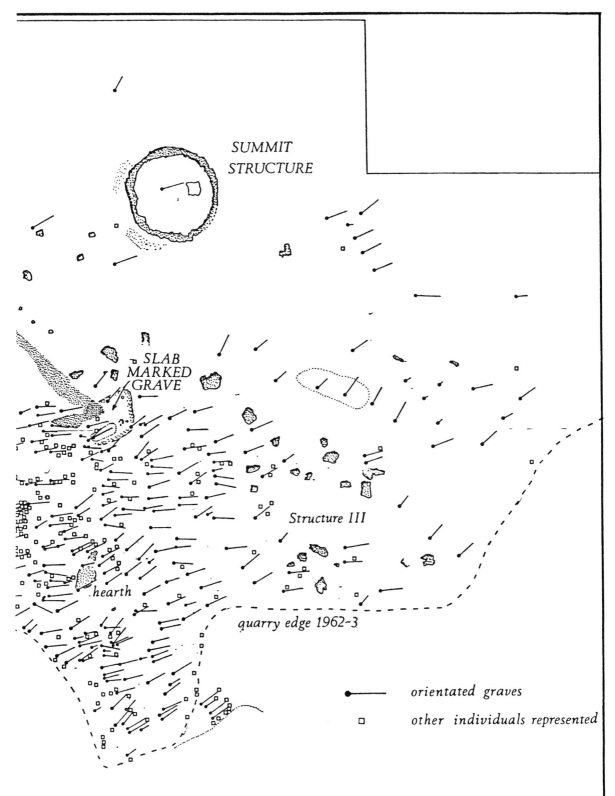

SUMMIT
STRUCTURE

SLAB
MARKED
GRAVE

Structure III

hearth

quarry edge 1962-3

●——— orientated graves

□ other individuals represented

its back (supine). Burials placed on their side occur at Cirencester, Lankhills, Ilchester and Cannington but are rather rare. More significant, however, may be the incidence of prone burials, bodies placed face down in the grave, which occur sporadically at Poundbury, Ilchester, Lankhills, Cirencester and Radley (Oxon.). They include the burials of adult males and females as well as some children. Whether the prone attitude denotes any special significance is not clear. The burials are relatively rich in grave goods and were not relegated to the limits of the burial areas. They are absent from the post-Roman cemeteries but do occur also in cemeteries of Anglo-Saxon date where evidence for live burial is suggestive of sacrificial interpretations. Another unusual rite found in late Roman cemeteries is decapitation. Heads had occasionally been neatly removed, usually after death, and replaced above the neck or positioned between or next to the feet of the skeleton (**70**). Such burials have been recorded

at Lankhills, Poundbury, Ilchester and Radley. At Lankhills, the decapitated burials tended to be located near either rich or ritually unusual graves, and it was concluded that the victims may have been sacrificial. However, at Poundbury the three decapitated bodies had been buried in an isolated position west of the main cemetery area, and an interpretation in terms of special treatment for selected individuals, possibly outcasts, might be more appropriate.

On the basis of the occurrence of numbers of grave goods, Late Roman cemeteries can be divided into two main groups: those cemeteries with significant numbers of grave goods and these which have produced very few (**71**). The types of objects deposited in graves included coins; ornaments such as brooches, bracelets, rings or beads, which could be worn by the corpse or placed next to the body (i.e. unworn); equipment such as knives, combs, boxes, spindle-whorls or weapons; hobnailed boots; vessels of pottery, glass or metal; and the remains of

70 *Decapitated skeleton within the cemetery at Ilchester. The detached head has been placed between the feet.*

71 *The occurrence of grave goods in late Roman and post-Roman cemeteries.*

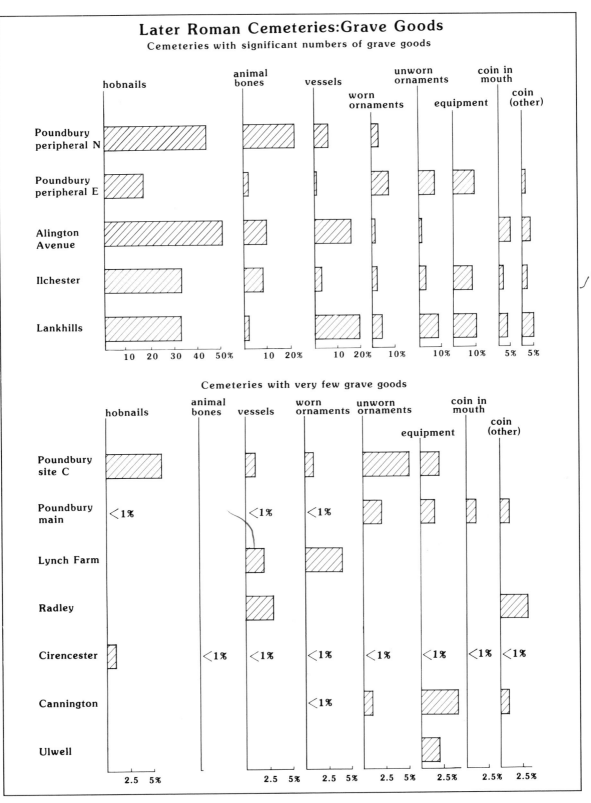

Later Roman Cemeteries:Grave Goods
Cemeteries with significant numbers of grave goods

joints of meat, eggshells or traces of beverages. In the terms of what these items may have signified to the burying population, various possible interpretations may be suggested. Some items may have been used to assist in attaining a neat appearance for the laid-out body (e.g. jewellery, combs) while others may have been deposited as offerings. These offerings may have been intended for use during the journey to an afterworld (especially a coin placed in the mouth, providing for Charon's fee to cross the Styx, and boots with hobnails), for the use of the individual in the afterlife (food, vessels and equipment), or as offerings to the gods. Suitable godly offerings might have included food, vessels, unworn ornaments, and coins placed in positions other than in the mouth. Finally the items deposited may have functioned only to denote the status or wealth of the individual buried. Such goods would include worn ornaments and some classes of equipment, especially certain tools and also weapons.

At Poundbury, the graves in the groups producing larger numbers of goods (see **67**, the peripheral N and E groups) were characterized by items related probably to use, either by the individual or the gods, in another world, or to the journey towards this goal: food offerings, vessels, equipment (knives and whorls) and unworn ornaments, as well as the commonly represented hobnail boots, although some worn ornaments were present also. By contrast, the graves of the main cemetery contained fewer goods, and these were mainly indicative of status (worn ornaments and some equipment). Also common in this sector were items related to the laying-out of the body (e.g. combs), and remains of neatly combed and arranged hairstyles came from some of the burials contained in the stone or lead coffins. The types of grave goods found in the other cemeteries represented in the histograms (see **71**) also cluster in ways that are similar.

We have seen that Late Roman burial practices differ quite markedly from those prevalent in the pre-Roman Iron Age. The rite became more standardized, supine inhumation or cremation being the preferred burial modes, and the regional variations so characteristic of the Iron Age can no longer be detected. However, by the Late Roman period the large inhumation cemeteries were not entirely uniform in their detailed characteristics. In particular, some cemeteries show a virtual absence of grave goods, while others contain many furnished graves. Some contain elaborate, apparently focal, graves and some burial grounds are characterized by graves arranged very neatly in parallel or slightly converging rows. It has been suggested that some of these variations may reflect the growing diversification of religious beliefs that took place in the later Roman period. The classical pagan rites were joined by mystery cults from the East, and gradually one of these, the practice of Christianity, began to achieve a more dominant position.

It is extremely difficult to define features in the archaeological data which can be taken as good evidence for Christianity, and several full-length books have recently been written on this subject. As far as the cemeteries are concerned, although no single characteristic can be taken as proof of Christian burial, there are a series of features that, if they occur together on one site, may be indicative of this. These features include strict west-east orientation, as burial with the head to the west would have allowed the individual to face Christ, assumed to be coming from the east at the time of the Second Coming, and the occurrence of burials of newly-born infants. Some pagan religions excluded babies from major burial grounds, but Christians believe that all individuals have equal spiritual status from birth. Early Christians also believed that the dead body should be maintained inviolate for the Second Coming, so features such as the avoidance of overlapping or disturbance between successive graves, and attempts at preserving the body, such as by plaster encasement, may also be indicative of Christian burial customs. Finally, the absence of grave goods may be associated with Christian beliefs. The body is believed to stand alone and offerings are not necessary, or allowed. However, goods related to the status of the individual *may* be found in Christian graves. The most telling evidence would be a Christian inscription found within a grave, but, with the exception of one disputed inscription on a lead coffin from Poundbury or the occasional occurrence of Christian symbols on items included in the grave (**73** and **colour plate 6**), these are not known from cemeteries in Britain.

In contrast to these indicators of possible Christian graveyards there are other features

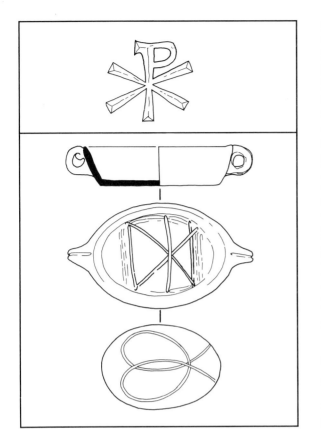

that are generally accepted as being connected with pagan beliefs. These include coins placed in the mouth, ornaments and equipment placed next to the body as offerings, the face-down burial rite, decapitation, north-south alignment of the grave and the frequent disturbance of earlier burials. Taking all these criteria into consideration, the cemetery that is most likely to have been Christian is Poundbury and the site with most pagan characteristics is the Ilchester west suburban graveyard. Other cemeteries which may contain Christian elements are Lankhills, Northover (east of Ilchester), a small cemetery east of the temple complex at Nettleton Scrub and the post-Roman cemeteries at Henley Wood, again next to a Roman temple, and at Cannington. Thus we come to the fascinating topic of the extent to which Christianity became established in Britain during the fourth to seventh centuries AD, and the theories and problems that are to be addressed in the second part of this book.

72 *(Above) Chi-rho symbol carved on a stone slab at Chedworth, Gloucestershire.*

73 *(Below) Possible chi-rho symbol incised inside the base of a dish from Lankhills.*

7

The Roman church

Christianity owes its birth to the impact of the historically recorded crucifixion and resurrection of Jesus Christ in the remote province of Palestine at a time around AD 33. The initial spread of the religion through the Mediterranean world during the first century is described in St Luke's Acts of the Apostles, and by the third century at the latest Christianity would have reached far-flung outliers of the empire such as Britain. At first Christian communities would have met in domestic surroundings for worship and fellowship, and communal purpose-built structures would not have existed until the fourth century AD. Initially the religion found most of its adherents in the towns and cities, but soon rich landowners were establishing private house-churches, on their country estates. In the early fourth century Christianity became the state religion within the Roman Empire, and, as the century progressed, its flourishing was both rapid and profound.

The historically ubiquitous Christian symbol of the simple cross, preferably depicted in a natural material, especially wood, was not generally employed until after AD 600. In the late Roman world, symbolism was more varied and less overt. A cross-like motif was provided by the chi-rho, a device which incorporated the first two letters of the Greek word *Christos*. This sign was sometimes accompanied by two further letters, the alpha and omega. These, being the first and last letters of the Greek alphabet, referred to the beginning and the end, recalling Revelation 1:8 'I am Alpha and Omega, saith the Lord God, which is and which was and which is to come'. In addition there were symbols based on plant and animal prototypes – the vine; the fish and dolphin; the peacock and the pomegranate, both of which were connected with the concept of immortality; doves; palm fronds; the Tree of Life; and finally, a sacred vessel (*cantharus*), visualized as the receptacle for the life-blood of Christ.

Portable Christian objects

Excavations over the last thirty years in England have led to the discovery of a whole series of buildings and structures that can be interpreted as basilicas, churches, chapels and fonts. These will form the main subject matter for this chapter, but before embarking upon that study it is instructive to consider the other, and more widespread, evidence for Christianity in Roman Britain. This includes objects, some of which have been known for several hundred years, which bear symbols of the type referred to above. The main categories are: large lead tanks; vessels and equipment of a domestic or liturgical nature; items of personal apparel or jewellery; and the components of buildings. The last group included inscribed examples of chi-rho or fish symbols on building stones, roof-tiles or bricks, of which only a handful of instances are known. More widespread are the known find-spots of hoards, which include groups of pewter or silver vessels and which represent most probably the property of wealthy families within the Christian community. Bowls, dishes, jugs and cups are most often present, along with a surprisingly high percentage of spoons. The latter may have been ascribed a liturgical use or have been exchanged as baptismal gifts (Christening spoons) or equally may have been standard table silver embellished with Christian signs and symbols.

One of the two large pewter hoards, that

from Appleshaw (Hants.), contained 32 vessels, one a bowl bearing a prominent, but secondarily incised, chi-rho and another a dish engraved at the time of its manufacture with a fan-tailed fish. Silver hoards also contained bowls, dishes and cups but were particularly noted for their spoon component. These large silver spoons were often decorated on the bowl with chi-rho symbols, alpha and omega, or the representation of a fish. In the hoards from Canterbury and Dorchester (Dorset) there were also enigmatic silver tools with one flat end and the other terminating in a prong. Suggestions for their possible use have included a toothpick, an implement for removing shellfish or snails from their shells or, in a more sacred context, the breaking and lifting of the Host during the celebration of Communion. These hoards are thought to be the domestic accoutrements of well-to-do Christians who buried their most valued possessions at a time of danger or unrest during the late fourth century, but the more recently discovered hoard of material from Water Newton may have been the property of a Christian community, in fact a rare deposit of actual church plate (**colour plate 10**).

Deposited some time in the middle of the fourth century, the Water Newton hoard contained three bowls, two jugs, two cups, a dish and a strainer, all of silver. Four pieces bore chi-rho symbols and in two cases these were flanked by alpha and omega. There were no spoons, but there was a series of leaf-shaped plaques in sheet silver. These were similar to the copper alloy leaves and feathers known from pagan temples in that they bore relief ribs and veining, but many of them were inscribed with chi-rho symbols, with or without the addition of the signs for alpha and omega. A single gold-sheet disc carried a similar device. Most of the leaves had been pierced to facilitate their attachment to a board, or to the wall of a building. The various inscriptions that occurred on some of the vessels included four distinct personal names and it seems likely that the group who deposited the hoard contained the members of more than one family. If the vessels had functioned as church plate, then the dish may have been used for the bread, the jug and strainer for preparation of the wine, and the two-handled cup as a container for the wine during consecration.

Single vessels, usually of pewter, have also been found to bear Christian symbols. Three pewter bowls from various rural and urban locations had chi-rho symbols on the underside of the base, while an example from Sutton, Isle of Ely, displayed a chi-rho between alpha and omega, as well as peacocks, on the flange of its octagonal rim. A larger form of stray vessel, the lead tanks, may have been used for baptismal purposes or as stoups or storage containers for holy water. Examples from Wiggonholt (Sussex), Icklingham, Ashton (Northants.) and Walesby (Lincs.) were decorated with chi-rho symbols, while six or so further examples, which may have been related, are plain. The tank from Walesby carried also a remarkable scene incorporating architectural elements and human figures, the possible representation of a baptismal ceremony. The final group of items of Christian significance includes a series of fourth-century strap-ends, adorned with naturalistic motifs such as the peacock, fish or Tree of Life, and a number of precious or base metal finger rings and pottery lamps carrying inscriptions such as VIVAS IN DEO, or the usual Christian symbols.

To a group of three lead caskets which contain chi-rho symbols within their decorative schemes may now be added a fragment of copper-alloy sheet-metal from Uley which formerly adorned a Christian casket (**colour plate 7**). This fragment had been folded into four and secreted in the remodelled shrine at the end of the fourth century. Careful study of the scenes executed in repoussé technique suggests that the subject matter included the following biblical narratives – Christ and the centurion, Matthew 8:5–14 (top left); Christ healing the blind man, John 9 (top right); Jonah reclining under the gourd, Jonah 4 (bottom left); and, at bottom right, the sacrifice of Isaac, Genesis 22. This fragment may have derived, in accordance with the continental parallels, from a box which would also have had scenes of a more classical and pagan nature. However, the selection of this particular portion by a worshipper could well indicate an act of Christian devotion.

Town and country churches

Late Roman churches have been the subject of much recent excavation and discussion. Most of the evidence is enigmatic or tentative and its evaluation has formed the subject matter for three books published since 1980. The known examples may be divided usefully into four groups: urban basilicas; rural churches; house-

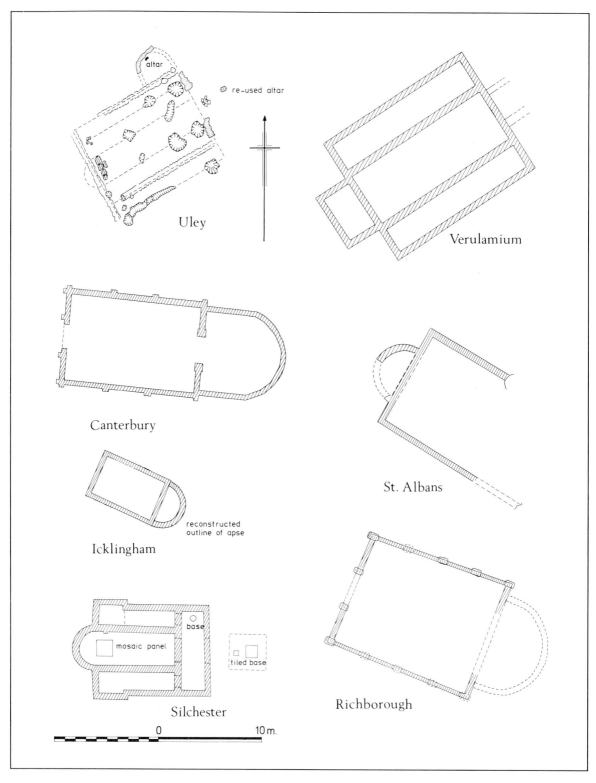

74 *Plans of some early churches in Britain.*

or estate-churches; and suburban or cemetery chapels. A selection of late Roman church plans is shown in **74**. In the late Roman period it was just as correct for the altar to be placed at the west end as in the east. West-east orientation for the church structure was preferred although, as can be seen from **74**, this was seldom exact. The buildings were rectangular in shape, sometimes with the addition of side aisles, and usually with an apsidal extension at the east or west end. The aisled building from the south-east quarter of Verulamium (St Albans; **74**, top right) possessed a square projection to the west and an eastern porch; it was identified quite plausibly as a small Christian church as early as the 1930s. At Canterbury, the large eastern apse of the first phase of St Pancras church was actually polygonal. Otherwise, it was roughly similar in plan, although oppositely aligned, to that of the second church plan from St Albans, that belonging to a probable church in an extramural location at Verulam Hill Fields. Inside the fort at Richborough (Kent) the plan of a large rectangular church has been reconstructed from a pattern of stone foundation blocks. These could have supported a timber superstructure and there may have been an eastern apse. The largest of the urban churches so far identified in Britain is that at Flaxengate, Lincoln. Here the postulated five-bay basilica possessed an eastern apse and, probably, a narthex across the western end. In plan this church is reflected, but on a lesser scale, by the building excavated south of the Forum at Silchester (**74**, lower left). Although long accepted as a Christian church, a recent reassessment of both its plan, and also particularly the dating, which places the period of use between the late third and mid-fourth centuries, has raised other possibilities. The building may be too early to have been a Christian church and the plan could have been suitable for the rituals connected with one of the other eastern mystery cults. However, the presence of the probable font base in front of the eastern entrance, and its parallels on other early church sites, would seem to uphold the Christian interpretation.

The examples of rural churches known from Icklingham (Suffolk) and Witham (Essex) are much smaller than the urban ones described above. At Icklingham (see **74**) the rectangular building is known from foundation trenches only and the eastern apse is conjectural, while the small church or chapel at Witham was a simple rectangular shell, possibly with two cells. The early church plan recovered at Uley was somewhat larger (see **74**, top left). A series of large post pits and a beam-slot cut through the demolished remains of the Roman stone temple were very conspicuous features and they were recognized at the time of excavation to have been the remains of the footings for one or more timber buildings. It was apparent also that these features were cut at a level which matched that of a roughly laid apsidal stone floor surviving above the wall foundations of the former north-western ambulatory of the Roman temple.

The suggested interpretation for this arrangement of features is that a five-bay double-aisled structure had been constructed over, and in exact alignment with, the demolished temple remains (see **74**, top left and **75**). One post pit and an associated levelling layer contained fragments from the Roman cult statue and a second, smaller, figure. In front of a central doorway was an area of stone paving, approached by a step over the robbed foundations of the Roman portico wall. This step had been made using a segment of a large Roman altar, depicting the god Mercury, but placed face downwards. Two joining fragments of the top of the same altar, and a second complete altar, which also bore a sculptured figure of Mercury (see **59**), had been placed in inverted positions within the paving of the apsidal feature which lay over the remains of the south-western ambulatory. The remains of drystone footings around part of this floor matched those of the façade described above and could have supported a timber apse or polygonal extension to the main building.

If the Uley building was a Christian church, then the linear setting of stone slabs centrally positioned at the south-western end could have supported an altar and, behind this, there may have been a small apse. However, no evidence for this putative apse was found, and if it had existed, any traces in this zone of the site would have been destroyed by ploughing. The timber basilica was constructed probably during the fifth century and may have survived into the sixth century AD. A tentative reconstruction of the building is shown in **75**, which shows a five-bay timber structure with simple window openings at clerestory level. The roof is covered

75 *Artist's reconstruction of the wooden basilica and banked enclosure at Uley (phase 7a).*

by wooden shingles and the gables ends are embellished with crossed finials. Beyond the central entrance, the side of the polygonal extension may be seen. Sources used during compilation of this drawing were the reconstruction of the late Roman church at Silchester, and in marked contrast, drawings of post-Roman timber halls. An asymmetrical extension of the type deduced for this building is, in a Christian context, most likely to have functioned as a baptistery, that is a baptismal tank or font. The basilica can be paralleled in Britain but the attached baptistery cannot. Several examples of separate baptisteries occur in close association with such churches, but attached baptisteries are known at present only from southern Europe. The church at Uley was surrounded by a timber-revetted bank with tower entrances.

Baptism

Detached baptisteries of fourth- and fifth-century date have been recognized in southern Britain and the plans of some of these are given in **76**. The evidence for late Roman baptism rests mainly on these traces of detached baptismal tanks or fonts. They were probably covered by insubstantial or temporary shelters and it has been deduced that the most probable form the ritual took would have been affusion. The act of affusion involves the pouring of water over the head and allowing it to dribble down the body; certainly such a style of baptism would have been more appropriate for the virtually outdoor ceremonies, which more often than not would have taken place in periods of inclement weather, than a rite of total immersion.

The existence of detached baptisteries in Britain was expounded first in the early 1970s when sets of pillar bases and a tank excavated at Richborough (Kent) were identified as the remains of a late Roman basilican church and free-standing baptistery, by comparing them with several examples known from the Rhine-Danube frontier. The font or baptismal cistern was hexagonal in shape, constructed of tiles and mortar, with six incurved faces, two of which had been blocked, perhaps for the provision of steps (see **76**). The exterior was faced with pink plaster and the inside of the basin had been plastered also.

It has been convincingly argued that the setting of tiles, covering 3.2 sq. m (34 sq. ft) and placed upon a flint plinth just east of the

entrance to the late Roman church at Silchester, may have supported a similar detached tank or font. A soakaway was located immediately to the west and the whole may have been covered by a light wooden enclosing structure (see **76**). A further detached baptismal tank has been excavated east of the church at Icklingham (Suffolk). This was apsidal in shape and provided with an internal step. The interior of the tank was lined with white plaster and immediately north of the baptistery was found a lead tank. This tank contained a group of iron objects: hinges, hinge-pins, nails and saw blades, which may indicate the dismantling of a light wooden shed or shelter.

It has been suggested above that the apsidal stone-paved extension attached to the northern corner of the timber basilican church at Uley may have functioned as such a baptistery. In a later phase, following the demise of the basilica, this portion of the building was the only area remodelled. A new perimeter wall was constructed, impinging slightly upon the paved floor of the former apse but also reusing it (see **76**). This wall was of drystone construction and incorporated fragments of reused painted wall plaster and mortar. The walls were of unknown height but were lined and faced most probably with a thick layer of white plaster. The remnants of these plaster facings were found spread southwards above the remains of the north-western temple ambulatory, and the survival of this debris indicates that the remodelled plaster-covered structure may have been one of the latest to have been used on the site. The simplest hypothesis would be that the remodelled apse replaced the attached baptistery in terms of location and function but that it now served as a free-standing structure: the detached baptistery for the stone churches to be described in the next chapter. The configuration of the remaining wall fragments and the outline of the floor suggest that the modified baptistery may have been octagonal in shape. Associated with the structure were three postholes, two of which may have been employed in the support of timbers designed to hold a temporary covering of cloth or leather, or even a flimsy but more permanent covering structure made of timber and wattle.

The octagonal shape of the Uley structure may be matched at no less than three further sites. Firstly, there is the octagonal fourth- to sixth-century font, constructed of tufa and

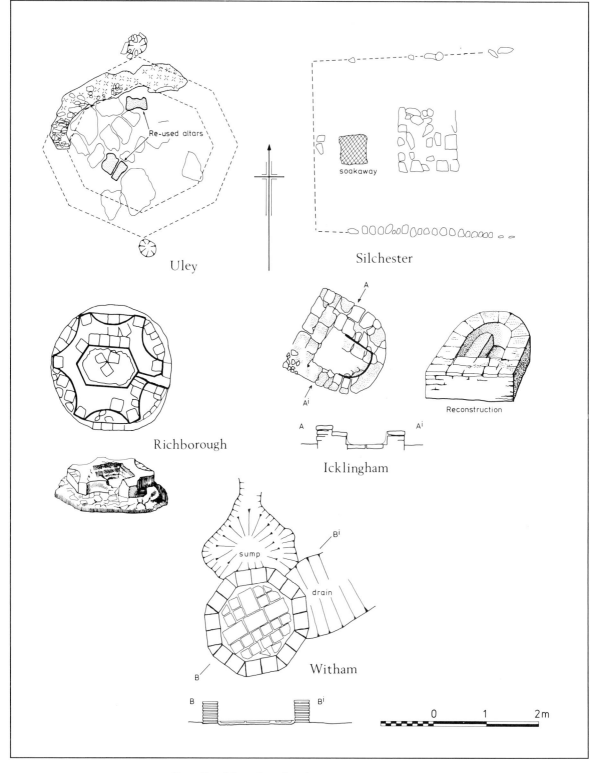

76 *Details of baptisteries from Roman Britain.*

possessing red plaster facings, found outside the eastern end of the cathedral at Cologne. A rather more rudimentary octagon, of three main phases, has been interpreted as a font at Ivy Chimneys, Witham (Essex) (see **75**). This tank was constructed of brick, rising from a floor made up of Roman tiles set in a composite cement. The two later phases incorporated marginal post-holes, which may have supported a covering shelter, and a sump lay adjacent to it. The structure lay on a site where a possible Iron Age shrine, a Roman temple and post-Roman buildings have been identified. Finally, in northern Gloucestershire, the octagonal spring-fed basin of the probable *nymphaeum* at Chedworth, may have been converted to use as a baptismal tank late in the fourth century. Certainly some of the marginal slabs were inscribed with chi-rho symbols at that time (see **72**). A theological context for the octagonal shape may be cited. Ideological links between baptism and death with Christ (see Colossians 2:12) are echoed by the provision of an octagon which expresses the co-resurrection of the baptismal candidate with Christ, who was raised from the dead on what the early church fathers called the eighth day, which was the first day of the new week.

House churches

The most convincing evidence for a Roman house church comes from Lullingstone in Kent where, in the villa itself, a pagan *nymphaeum* was replaced in the late fourth century by a suite of two rooms, cut off from the rest of the house and supplied with a new exterior entrance. Both rooms were adorned with wall-paintings which featured chi-rho monograms and human figures with their arms outstretched in prayer: the so-called *orantes* attitude which is often connected with early Christianity. The other candidates for the label 'house church' or 'estate chapel' include a series of villa sites where two rooms of some architectural pretension were connected by an open arch, and floored with a continuous mosaic of the most elaborate nature. The most controversial of these sites is Littlecote (Wilts.) where the very remarkable pavement, first discovered and recorded in 1728, has been re-excavated and restored in recent years (**77**). The larger rectangular room possessed a western extension with three apses, an arrangement known in classical terms as a *triconch*. The building, with

an associated bath suite, was separate from the main house and has been accepted by most scholars as a religious building. The mosaic in the rectangular hall featured *canthari* (wine containers) (as **90**) flanked by sea beasts, dolphins (as **91**) and panthers, while that in the principal three-lobed room depicted Orpheus, with shell patterns occupying the three apses. However, Orpheus was shown in the guise of Apollo and was surrounded by scenes taken from Orphic myth. Therefore the excavators have suggested that the building functioned as a pagan Orphic cult room. The problem is that the Orphic mystery cult shared many characteristics with early Christianity. In the late Roman period, some Christians considered Orpheus and Apollo to be saviour-gods similar to Christ and the mosaic at Littlecote could therefore have been commissioned by a family of Christian persuasion.

Whilst the Christian symbolism at Littlecote, the *canthari* and dolphins, is of a general nature, other mosaics bore less ambiguous motifs, and these have been promoted as evidence for a group of house churches, all in Dorset. However, the mosaics also contain scenes from classical myth and it has been pointed out that they may reflect adherence to pagan beliefs by families purporting to be Christian. At Frampton an apsed room with side-chamber and narthex was probably a dining room. The mosaics depicted Bacchus (in the side-chamber), a horseman spearing a lioness, surrounded by dolphins, and, in the apse, a *cantharus* and a chi-rho contained in a roundel. A western room in the villa at Fifehead Neville contained a mosaic showing a *cantharus* encircled by seven fish and four dolphins, and a hoard found nearby included two silver rings decorated with chi-rho motifs. Finally, at Hinton St Mary (Dorset), the mosaic occupied a double room which was probably a public chamber, but its subject matter strongly suggests the existence of a Christian chapel elsewhere in the establishment (**colour plate 8**). Again, pagan themes were present, although the scene of Bellerophon spearing the Chimaera could be seen to represent the triumph of good over evil. The corner figures of the main mosaic may have been the four evangelists in the guise of wind-gods, whilst in the centre, the head of a dark-eyed clean-shaven man with penetrating gaze superimposed on a chi-rho monogram, was flanked by a pair of pomegranates. This is

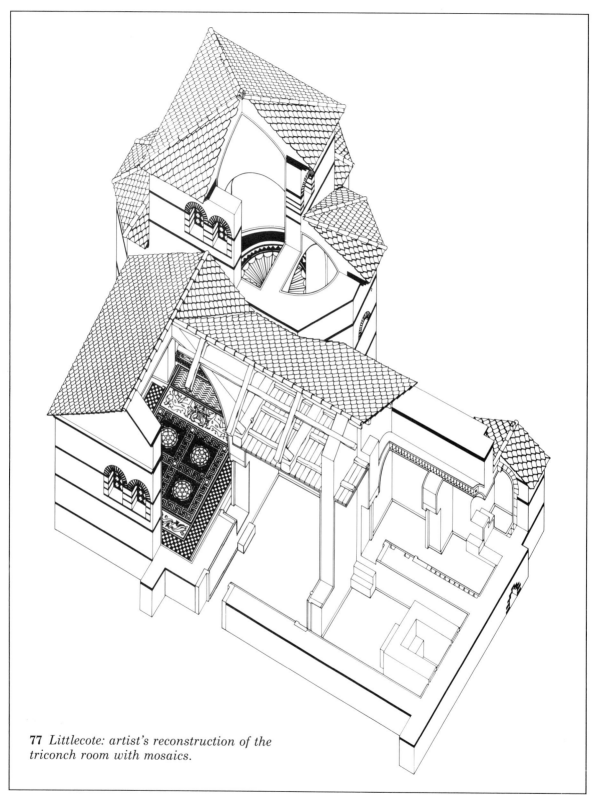

77 *Littlecote: artist's reconstruction of the triconch room with mosaics.*

generally accepted as a portrait of Christ, one of the earliest from the entire Roman Empire. To the earliest church, any visual image of Christ would have been viewed as a graven image, and one that could be brushed by human feet deplored as a violation. To the fourth-century Christian communities of Dorset however it must have been not only acceptable but highly valued and venerated.

Cemetery churches

The fourth and last group of late Roman Christian churches to be considered are the chapels found in major cemeteries outside the walls of Roman towns. On the continent of Europe a large body of research has demonstrated that many Roman and early medieval churches, and often the sites of medieval towns, developed from the focus provided by the shrine or mausoleum of a Roman martyr located in such extramural cemeteries. Some of the best known examples are from Mainz, Bonn, Xanten, Trier and Bordeaux. In Britain several extramural cemeteries associated with towns have been excavated in recent years, and some were seen to have a Christian character. At Poundbury, amongst the graves of the very extensive burial ground there, was a series of small rectangular stone-built structures which contained burials and may have functioned as mausolea or cemetery chapels of the *martyrium* or *memoria* type (**78**). Decorated plaster indicates that some were walled and roofed, but others may have been mere enclosures surrounded by low walls or shelters with roofs supported on piers or pillars. In contrast to the continental evidence, none of these chapels developed into a church and by the early post-Roman period the area had been taken over for domestic use. However, on the other side of the Roman town of Dorchester, the early Saxon church of Fordington lay on the site of another cemetery belonging to the Roman town. This was a mixed cemetery but it may have contained Christian burials of particular importance, possibly housed in stone structures. Certainly there are hints of the former presence of Roman masonry below the Saxon church itself.

Outside the Roman town of Colchester there was a cemetery similar to that at Poundbury, on the site known as Butt Road (**79**). Associated with the cemetery was a building over 20 m (66 ft) long and 5 m (16 ft) wide, of aisled construction and possessing a small eastern apse.

A ritual pit near the eastern end is known to have been associated with a primary grave, perhaps that of a martyr or Christian leader, while outside the western end lay a timber structure containing a setting of tiles. The latter could possibly represent the remains of a baptismal tank similar to those discussed above (p. 103). Another extramural cemetery that appears to be similar to the one at Poundbury has been identified at Northover, just across the river from the East Gate at Ilchester. Traces of masonry recorded there amongst the grave outlines may belong to mausolea or chapels like those at Poundbury and, interestingly, an adjacent mound became the site for an important minster church during the Saxon period. At St Albans, the extramural church excavated in Verulam Hills Field has already been noted (p. 101). This was located within a cemetery area, while just to the north, on a prominent hill, is the probable site of the *martyrium* of St Alban, who was put to death in the early third century. This shrine almost certainly lay within the Roman cemetery known to underlie the existing cathedral. Furthermore, it was around this holy focus that the medieval town developed, leaving the Roman city derelict in the valley below.

Although these examples of extramural church locations may seem to reflect the pattern known from Europe, the most recent research is beginning to indicate that in fact more of the Saxon and early Medieval churches in British towns developed directly from late Roman churches within the original city walls. There are many cases where churches are known to have grown up in proximity to the former public buildings of Roman towns, and especially the *forum*. Examples of such a process include St Peter, Cornhill, in London, St Paul-in-the-Bail in Lincoln, the church of Holy Saviour below Canterbury cathedral and Edwin's seventh-century church at York; similar developments also occurred at Colchester, Exeter, Gloucester and Chichester. Whether these medieval churches had late Roman antecedents remains to be tested and this is one of the next major tasks for archaeologists studying the early Christian period. The hypothesis of intra-mural continuity is also upheld on the continent, in particular by the recent programmes of research undertaken at Tours, Trier and Geneva.

To end this brief study of the Roman church

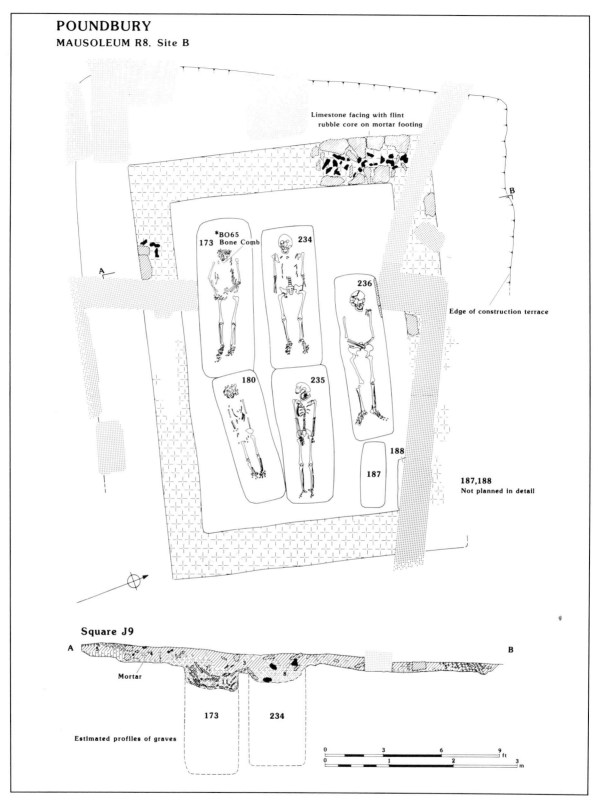

POUNDBURY
MAUSOLEUM R8, Site B

Limestone facing with flint
rubble core on mortar footing

B

*BO65
173   Bone Comb   234

236

Edge of construction terrace

180   235

188

187

187,188
Not planned in detail

A

Square J9

A   5   B

Mortar
7   3
11   8

173   234

Estimated profiles of graves

0   3   6   9 ft
0   1   2   3 m

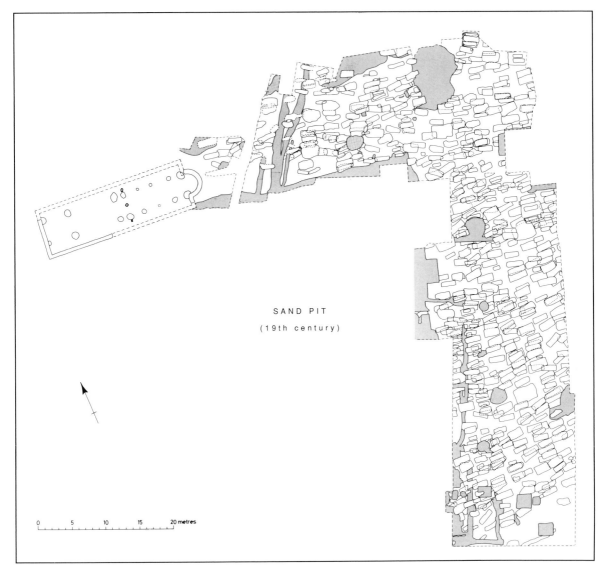

78 *(Left) Plan of one of the mausolea in the Poundbury cemetery.*

79 *(Above) Plan of the church and cemetery at Butt Road, Colchester.*

in Britain it is necessary to consider a matter which relates very positively to our themes of site reuse. This is the inclusion of pagan sculpture and defaced altars within the fabric of early Christian buildings. At the pagan Temple of Mithras, Walbrook, London, the sculptures were removed in the mid-fourth century. The larger pieces were dismembered and then the pieces were buried in groups at salient points in the building. The structure may have been thus converted to function as a Christian church. The church construction levels at Icklingham sealed a pit which contained items possibly deriving from a pagan shrine: decorated roof tiles and a limestone pillar, along with human skulls and bones. At Uley fragments of pagan cult statues and defaced Roman altars were incorporated into the fabric of the timber basilica, and somewhere within it may have been secreted the head of the major statue of Mercury. Certainly this head was accessible for later ritual deposition beneath the subsequent stone church which was constructed on the same site (see below, p. 117).

109

8

The early Christian church

In southern and eastern Britain the flourishing Christian church of the late Roman period probably continued in some form into the poorly-documented first decades of the fifth century. Recent research and analysis suggest that the decay of the towns and their Roman-style economy was both abrupt and terminal. As discussed above, the Roman church appears to have been strongest in the towns, so some transformation of the religion along with the decline of the town are to be expected. Little is known, however, of any such transformation because by the middle of the fifth century the eastern zone had been overrun by the Anglo-Saxons who introduced their own pagan cults, along with a new set of deities and associated symbolism, from northern Europe. Most evidence for the pagan religion derives from vast cemeteries of graves which contained burials accompanied by weapons, personal equipment, rich jewellery and all the exotic paraphernalia of warriors, wealthy landlords and kings. Thus paganism held sway once more, at least until reconversion of the English, which was initiated by the mission instigated by St Augustine in AD 597.

The Saxon incursion did not reach south-western Britain, Wales, Scotland or Ireland and in these areas the seeds of Christianity sown in Roman Britain continued to bear fruit through the fifth and sixth centuries. There is evidence that the Roman diocesan structure survived into the post-Roman period, with bishops and priests being mentioned on memorial stones of the fifth and sixth centuries. Such stones have been found in southern Scotland, and in north-west Wales, as at Aberdaron (Gwynedd) where the memorial inscription reads 'VERIACIUS PBR [presbiter] HIC IACIT':

'here liest the priest Veriacius'. Christianity in western Britain and Ireland flourished during the fifth and sixth centuries and was spurred on by new and direct contacts with France and, probably, the eastern Mediterranean. These contacts are demonstrated most clearly by the occurrence of sherds of pottery vessels, some of them bearing Christian symbols, which had been imported from the Mediterranean world to be used on the early religious and stronghold sites of south-western Britain and the Welsh coast. A further boost to Christian development was provided by the flowering of monasticism in the seventh century. The concept of monasticism had its origin in the desert areas of the eastern Mediterranean and north Africa and had been introduced to south-western Britain probably by the late fifth century. There were new foundations in South Wales and Ireland in the sixth century. By the late sixth century the monastic mode had spread to north-western Britain and finally, the seventh century saw the culminating glory of the early Christian monastic development, in Northumbria.

Chapels and churches

The archaeological evidence for Christianity in the Celtic west consists of the memorial stones referred to above together with cemeteries, some of which were associated with chapels, and the monastic sites themselves. No churches dated to the fifth or sixth centuries have survived in the west, but they were probably small oratories constructed of timber, similar to those excavated examples which are dated to the seventh century. The earliest stone churches are drystone beehive cells with corbelled roofs. Although none of these can be dated to earlier than AD 700, they must represent an ancient

and native tradition. The best known stone oratories are those of Gallerus type. Two such buildings on the monastic site of Skellig Michael (Co. Kerry) may be of eighth-century date, but the Gallerus oratory itself (also in Co. Kerry) (80) is undatable and may be as late even as the twelfth century. The elegant curved profile may be due to the imitation in stone of a cruck-built timber building, and the butterfly gable finials and lintelled doorways of other early stone churches may also be copies of wooden prototypes.

The preceding timber oratories are best represented by two excavated examples, one from Ireland and one from south-west Scotland. At Church Island (Co. Kerry) an unenclosed cemetery became the site for a small timber oratory supported by posts (see 82). There was a circular living cell nearby and this phase may date from the seventh century. Possibly in the early eighth century the timber structure was replaced by a larger stone chapel, surrounded by more burials, and the cell was also rebuilt in stone. A very similar sequence was demonstrated by excavation at Ardwall Island (Kirkcudbrightshire) where a timber oratory, burials

80 *The oratory at Gallerus, Co. Kerry.*

and post-holes for a possible corner-post shrine were constructed over a cemetery of the late fifth or sixth century, and replaced later by a stone chapel of larger dimensions (see 82). A third example (see 82) has been excavated at Carnsore (Co. Wexford). As monasticism developed, timber chapels of this type would have occurred within monastic enclosures, along with cells for the monks, specialist buildings such as a guesthouse or refectory, and agricultural structures, workshops and arable plots.

From Wales, one candidate for an early church is the putative oratory that underlies the tenth-century chapel beneath the present church of Ynys Seiriol (Puffin Island), Anglesey. The church occupies a large oval enclosure and there are three or four stone cells of unknown date. At Llandegai a timber oratory was associated with an early Christian cemetery next to the Neolithic henge monuments, while at Burry Holms (Glamorgan) a timber chapel below the stone church may have been eleventh century in date. The first phase of an enclosure wall was of turf, revetted by small stones, and was later surmounted by a palisade which may have been contemporary with the timber chapel. The best example of an early oratory site from the south-west is the hermitage chapel on St Helens, Isles of Scilly. The earliest structures here were a drystone circular hut, possibly of the seventh or eighth century, associated with an oratory constructed from large stones and containing a cavity for relics. This chapel was certainly earlier than the twelfth century, but could not be dated more closely.

The reuse of Roman temples

In south-western England it is instructive to consider whether any similar structures were sited on the existing religious sites in that area. In this zone, which lies beyond the direct influence of Saxon settlement, the religious sites would have been the late Romano-Celtic temples and house-churches, and the cemeteries and mausolea of the late Roman and post-Roman periods. The methodical excavations undertaken on many such sites have provided information that can be interpreted as demonstrating such a development. At Uley there were four major phases of restructuring and continued religious use after the demise of the developed Roman temple buildings, and on several other sites there is substantial evidence for the continuance of religious usage into the fifth century and beyond. In some cases the modifications may have been effected by those of pagan persuasion, but in others early Christian connections can be suggested with some certainty.

At Uley towards the end of the fourth century, the front of the aggrandized stone temple fell or had to be demolished. Most likely, subsidence above the fillings of the deep early Roman ditch and votive pit eventually caused the foundations of the north-eastern corner of the temple to give way. The portico would have collapsed and, along with it, the main superstructure of the *cella* appears to have been reduced to a heap of rubble and fallen roof tiles. Only the north-western and south-western ambulatories survived. Apparently the late Roman worshippers did not possess the means or motivation to reconstruct the edifice to its former glory, for, almost immediately, the rubble was cleared away. Some of it was scattered over the remains of the building to the

south-west, where spreads of rubble and dark soil containing votive debris survived in hollows above the fillings of the robber trenches. The surviving ambulatories were restored, modified and extended to provide a unique L-shaped building which possessed at least four rooms. The two former ambulatories were divided from each other by a blocking wall, the south-eastern end of the south-west ambulatory was converted into a small square room, and a rectangular timber-framed annexe was built over a former opening from the ambulatory and on part of the previous floor area of the fallen *cella*. Evidence of burning, and deposits containing votive objects in quantity, indicated a continuing religious function.

The surviving ambulatories must have been re-roofed and some of the former arches between them and the fallen *cella* blocked. The timber-framed annexe was possibly faced in reused stone blocks from the temple, but equally may have been of wattle-and-daub construction. Traces of the other temple walls were probably still visible, and it is suggested that some of these may have been used to support a low wall defining an area in front of the newly-built annexe. Such an extraordinary and makeshift structure may have been built with great speed, and for a very specific and pressing purpose. This purpose is most likely to have been for the furtherance of the flourishing, and economically beneficial, cult of Mercury and above all, to provide safe and appropriate shelter for the cult statue. It can be suggested that offerings continued to be presented in the north-western ambulatory and the adjacent timber-framed annexe, whilst the statue itself may have survived in its former position, or have been re-erected, either within the new annexe, or within the safe confines and darkness of the newly-constructed square room at the end of the former south-western ambulatory. We have little knowledge of the surroundings in this period, although the timber-framed buildings to the north may have been still in use, providing shelter and services for the visiting pilgrims. Thus the cult of Mercury continued to thrive, and on the evidence of coinage, for another generation the cult image may have been carefully curated and venerated within its asymmetrical makeshift shrine.

Within the literature concerning Roman temples in Britain, examples of converted temple ruins are seldom described. However, it needs to be appreciated that the processes of extension, modification, demolition and reconstruction that may be demonstrated for English churches between the eleventh and sixteenth centuries are likely to have occurred just as commonly in Roman temples between the first and fifth centuries. The reasons for the lack of recognition of such processes are twofold. Firstly, there is a dearth of detailed twentieth-century temple excavations, adequately recorded and published, and secondly, temple chronologies have been compressed all too often, due to misinterpretations of coin evidence. In other words, structural phases which may have occurred in the fifth century or beyond have been squashed into the late Roman period (up to AD 402), when coins were still current. Thus, in order to find parallels for the situation at Uley, we must look to the continent of Europe, where traces of blocking walls within temple ambulatories and late conversions have been noted more often. In particular, at Civaux, Vienne, the temple possessed blocking walls within the ambulatory and an early Christian church was constructed along its south side. With all these points in mind, it is worth reconsidering evidence from some of the more detailed and extensive excavations that have taken place on Romano-Celtic temple sites in Britain. Initially, only examples of late fourth- or early fifth-century conversion or modification, probably executed in a continuing pagan context will be considered. Discussion of coincident structures newly built in the post-Roman period will follow later.

At Bath the inner precinct of the great temple of Sulis Minerva was resurfaced many times and continued in use well into the fifth century, if not beyond into the early sixth. Detailed evidence for any late modifications to the temple itself is not available, but the recent excavations within the inner precinct demonstrated the existence of a small room converted from part of the portico to the sacred reservoir. This building incorporated reused column drums at its corners and entrance and dated probably from the late fourth century. In two subsequent phases, probably extending well into the fifth century, timber structures were present within the precinct and built against the walls of the portico. By this time the temple itself was in a delapidated state, but the upper part of the Roman reservoir building was not demolished until the sixth century or even a little later. The excavators suggested that the room converted from part of the reservoir portico may have functioned as a small shrine.

From a modern and impeccably recorded excavation, we now turn to the less recent but still brilliantly executed programme of research mounted in the 1920s at Lydney Park by Mortimer Wheeler. The importance of the post-Roman earthwork at Lydney has been noted and reconsidered by scholars, but remarkably little attention has been paid to the construction sequence displayed by the temple plan itself. A complex and extraordinary building history was conflated by the excavator to a system of three main periods spanning only 40 years in all. A more expansive interpretation of the coin evidence than that put forward by the excavator would suggest, not only that the first temple may have originated well before the date of AD 364 suggested by the excavator but that the building remained in use, albeit in a modified form, further into the fifth century than he had envisaged. The plans of the Period I 'classical' temple and the reconstructed, more Romano-Celtic version, of Wheeler's Period II have been illustrated above (see **29**). This second temple probably does date to the later fourth century and the plan shows that the ambulatory was divided from the entrance area by a peculiar system of blocking walls which may have belonged to more than one phase of conversion. The *cella* floor was relaid to include a fine fish mosaic and a funnel to receive votive offerings and, at round about the same time, three L-shaped screen walls were erected within the ambulatory to form 'side-chapels'. In an even later phase of refurbishment (Period III), new mosaics were laid in two of the chapels and the whole ambulatory floor was raised. This phase must belong to the fifth century AD, and the small rectangular room projecting eastwards from the entrance façade of the temple, which produced no dating evidence, may well belong to this last (or even later) phase. Although the excavator had termed the sub-division within the ambulatory 'chapels', he did not view them in any way as evidence for Christianization. He felt that their purpose may have been that of subsidiary shrines, areas set aside for different categories amongst the worshipping population, or cubicles provided to accommodate ritual dreamers. Whatever their specific purpose, the process of increasing compartmentalization can be seen to echo the situation at Uley, although at Lydney this was in a temple that had not yet finally collapsed.

At Maiden Castle an oval hut with stone foundations, located south of the Romano-Celtic temple, has now been interpreted as a post-Roman shrine (see 8). As at Lydney, it

is also instructive to peruse the history of the temple building itself, as provided by the records of the excavator. The latest repair of the temple floor, incorporating reused roofing slabs, sealed coins which included very late issues; further examples of such coins were found, amongst others, upon this floor and nearby. Again as at Lydney, the implication must be that the temple continued in use well into the fifth century. No evidence of blocking walls was recovered but further 'compartments' were provided, firstly by the oval shrine, which may have been at least in part contemporary with the continuing use of the temple, and

81 *Nettleton: plan of the octagonal temple in its main final phase, with inserted walls blocking alternate segments of the interior. The resulting layout would have resembled a cross. The shaded stonework relates to a later stage of use.*

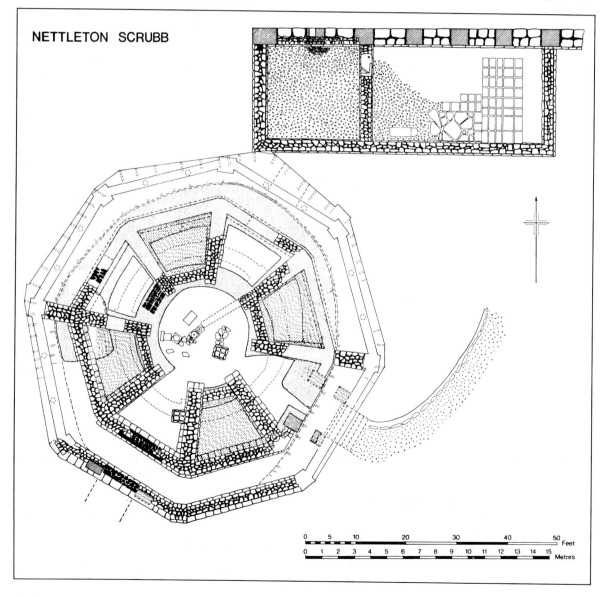

NETTLETON SCRUBB

secondly, possibly, by the so-called 'priest's house' which contained no dating evidence and, according to the plans, was of two phases. The primary room was of similar size to the portico shrine at Bath and to the late projecting eastern room at Lydney. Indeed, as a separate structure, it recalls also the late rectangular buildings located outside the temples at Brean and Lamyatt which are to be considered below.

Another temple which underwent a remarkable sequence of modification and compartmentalization in its later phases is the shrine of Apollo at Nettleton. The enlarged octagonal temple with its colonnaded ambulatory was modified, probably in the early to mid-fourth century, by the insertion of a series of blocking walls (81). These were built across alternate outer chambers of the octagonal *cella* structure such that a new central space of cruciform plan was formed. This space was refloored but there was no evidence for any continuing access to the sealed chambers. Largely on the basis of this cruciform plan, the excavator, Wedlake, argued that the temple had been converted to provide a Christian church. Subsequently, following a partial collapse of the *cella* vault, an improvised room incorporating reused column bases and voussoirs was constructed across the north-western portion of the former *cella*. Evidence provided by a single coin suggests that this room was constructed after AD 360 and finds from its floor indicated a continuing religious, but pagan, use.

The adjacent 'Post-Shrine Homestead', occupying the other half of the former *cella* and some of the outer chambers, was assigned to a later phase, but on the evidence of the published sections there seems no reason why both groups of occupation material should not have been contemporary. The 'homestead' layers produced coins of the very late fourth century and there can be no doubt that the whole complex continued to flourish well into the fifth century and possibly longer still. The case for the existence of a mid-fourth-century cruciform church remains unproven, but the process of compartmentalization and the provision of 'secret' rooms can now be seen to have occurred elsewhere: at Bath and Lydney, as well as at Uley, usually it seems in a continuing pagan context. Finally, no discussion of modified temples can be complete without reference to the octagonal example on Pagans Hill where a three-sided structure or screen was in

some way reconstituted or inserted in the late fourth century or beyond, and religious observance can be attested in the earlier Anglo-Saxon period. The ruined building was still in use during the medieval period and there may have been some continuing memory of its former character even in modern times.

The first Saxon churches

We may turn now to the examples of buildings that were built as new free-standing structures next to the sites of Romano-Celtic temples. The small buildings outside the Roman temples at Brean Down and Lamyatt Beacon are simple rectangular structures with eastern entrances (82). The building at Brean was constructed towards the end of the fourth century, or a little later. It was built without mortar from material robbed from the temple, and wear of the floor suggested a long period of use. The single room contained a hearth and small objects indicative of domestic occupation. But the excavator, ApSimon, was aware of the problems associated with such an interpretation: 'why was it built when a building of similar area could have been obtained by walling off part of one of the annexes or part of the ambulatory? If an unencumbered site was desired, use of the corner formed by the south wall of the ambulatory and the east wall of the south annexe would have saved half the work. This refusal to make use of standing structures and the choice of a different orientation look like a deliberate rejection of what had gone before.' In the light of the discovery of a similar building at Lamyatt, a religious function is preferred, but whether both or either served to house Christian or pagan worshippers cannot be ascertained. The structure excavated at Lamyatt (see 82) could not be dated closely, but may have been built with materials looted from the temple. It post-dated one of a series of nine burials of antlers and may or may not have been contemporary with the post-Roman cemetery located immediately north of it. In terms of date, these two buildings are likely to have been of fifth-, or possibly sixth-century date, although the nearby cemetery on the Brean sand cliff continued in use until the seventh or eighth century. In terms of function and date, they may belong more fittingly to our group of compartmentalized late Roman shrines discussed above. Such rooms may be viewed as further compartments which became separated

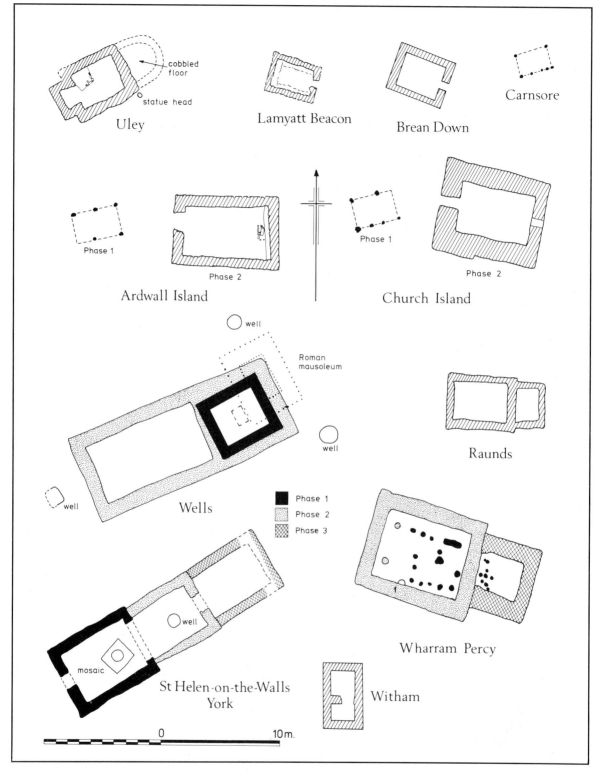

82 *Plans of post-Roman rectangular shrines and early Saxon churches.*

from the former temple building and they can be compared indirectly with the eastern room at Lydney which was attached to the temple itself.

These rectangular buildings are smaller than the earliest known early Christian stone chapels or oratories of the Celtic west such as the buildings at Church Island and Ardwall Island (see **82** and p. 111). However, as we have seen above, these were preceded by smaller shrines in timber which better match in size the rectangular buildings at Brean and Lamyatt. The timber shrines date from the seventh century, although that on Ardwall Island may have been constructed a little earlier. The Celtic stone versions may have been inspired by influence from Anglo-Saxon churches in England and they may be viewed as cemetery-based *memoriae* or *martyria*: cult-shrines associated with the graves of prominent local Christians. Any similar function for the Brean and Lamyatt buildings cannot be argued on the present evidence, but the stone structure at Uley, with its evidence for a western cell and a subsidiary eastern apse can be compared with the earliest Christian buildings further east: the churches of Anglo-Saxon England.

In the late sixth or early seventh century the timber basilica at Uley was dismantled and was replaced by a much smaller structure in stone. This new building was erected over the former north-eastern corner of both the basilica and of the preceding temple, and directly over the much earlier post-and-pit structure that had occupied the hollow over the deep Iron Age ditch (**83**, structure VIII). The structure was of two main phases: initially there was a simple rectangular two-celled building, possibly with an entrance midway along the eastern side; and, in a later phase, a larger structure, extended by the addition of an apse at the north-eastern end. The doorway may have been moved to the south-western end at this stage. The building is interpreted as a two-cell chapel, initially with an altar at the 'west' end. When the structure was increased in size the altar would then have been moved to the apsidal 'east' end and thus the orientation was reversed. This second phase of construction may have followed very rapidly upon the first. The building would have been tall, with a roof of used Roman stone tiles and round-headed windows located high in the walls (**84**). Possible voussoirs from such a window were found in the rubble lying

above the weathered floor of the structure. Only the cobbled floor of the apse survived. The superstructure may have been flimsy in nature or founded on horizontal beams; its wall may have been faced with stone; certainly Roman building materials must have been still available in abundance. The apse roof may have been shingled and its apex would have rendered the high east window architecturally inappropriate; this window might have been replaced by a lower east window in the apse wall. The later church is shown with a string course, and other architectural embellishments may have existed.

The presence of red-streaked window glass which can be dated to the seventh to ninth centuries AD provided a date for this building, thus suggesting the existence of a sophisticated church in a surprisingly rustic setting. Alternatively the 'window' glass may have been set originally within a piece of furniture or box. In a Christian context, this could have been an altar or a reliquary.

Both phases of church construction were accompanied by the deliberate burial of parts of the dismembered Roman cult statue. Two portions of the legs were incorporated into the foundations for the original north-eastern wall, and the head of Mercury was deposited in a pit just outside the eastern junction of chapel and apse. It is interesting to consider where these statue fragments may have been in between the act of dismembering the statue, an event which must have occurred prior to the construction of the timber basilica, and the construction of the stone church. The leg fragments, which were fairly weathered, may have been recovered from Roman demolition rubble, or from the packing around posts supporting the basilica at the time of its destruction. However, the statue head was crisp and totally unweathered. Indeed it does not seem to have been exposed at all to the elements, and may have been protected by a cloth or bag. The implication may be that the statue head had been retained, preserved and, presumably, venerated during the lifetime of the timber basilica. The head may have been placed in a recess within the basilica, hidden in a chest or even placed or sealed inside the altar itself. Christian doctrine has often attempted to subsume pagan elements rather than eradicate them, and the cult of the head which was so widespread in the Celtic world is known to have been reflected both in

117

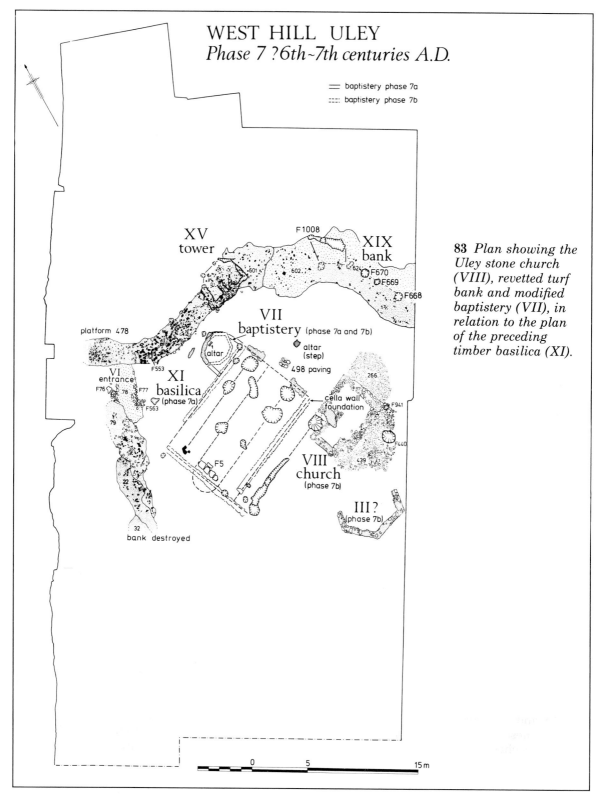

WEST HILL ULEY
Phase 7 ?6th~7th centuries A.D.

══ baptistery phase 7a
⋮⋮⋮ baptistery phase 7b

XV
tower

F1008

XIX
bank

601

602

624
F670
F669

F668

platform 478

VII
baptistery (phase 7a and 7b)

altar
altar
(step)

498 paving

VI
entrance

F553

266

F76
78 F77

XI
basilica
(phase 7a)

F563

cella wall
foundation

F941

79

F5

F440

22

VIII
church
(phase 7b)

439

32
bank destroyed

III ?
(phase 7b)

0   5   15 m

83 Plan showing the Uley stone church (VIII), revetted turf bank and modified baptistery (VII), in relation to the plan of the preceding timber basilica (XI).

84 *Artist's reconstruction of the stone church at Uley in its final phase.*

medieval church art and the cult of relics. However, the head of Mercury himself may have seemed too dangerous and profane an item to the early Christians, but they did not possess sufficient courage to destroy it, as instead it was now carefully hidden by burial next to the new sacred focus (in pit F941, see **83**). Alternatively the head may have been rescued by individuals of pagan leanings and buried secretly next to the new Christian shrine, or, more radically, the head may have been perceived or presented as an image of Christ himself, or a local saint or martyr.

The plan of the possible stone church at Uley may be compared with those of the earliest known Anglo-Saxon churches of eastern England. These were small timber chapels like those excavated at Wharram Percy (Yorkshire) (see **82**) and Thetford St Michael (Norfolk). Some of these were encased later by stone-walled churches which were of one or two cells. Early stone churches recently excavated include that of Wharram Percy, as well as Raunds (Northants.), Wells (Somerset) and St

Helen-on-the-Walls, York (see **82**). The last two were erected over foci of Roman date: a mausoleum at Wells and a mosaic roundel at York. At St Helen-on-the-Walls the mosaic roundel, depicting a female face, belonged probably to a corridor within a town-house (and not a house-church as has been suggested by some scholars), but the excavator concluded that 'it may be that the rediscovery of the mosaic inspired the erection of the first church and its dedication' (Magilton, 1980). All these simple stone churches date from the eighth to tenth centuries but seem to provide the best group of parallels for the stone building at Uley. Simple buildings with an early eastern apse are also well known in the Anglo-Saxon east, ranging from St Paul-in-the-Bail, Lincoln, located within the former Roman forum, to Angmering in Sussex.

These observations bring us full circle to the arguments advanced in the last chapter concerning the location of Saxon churches over the focal public buildings of the former Roman towns. Although in most of these cases we cannot discern the scale or nature of activities, religious or otherwise, on these sites in the fifth to seventh centuries, the frequency of these church locations does seem to indicate more than coincidence. The best sequence so far unravelled is that within the former Roman forum at Lincoln. Late Roman burials within the courtyard of the forum were succeeded by an apsidal church of unknown date, but earlier than the seventh century. Above this lay a mausoleum containing a burial richly provided with a hanging-bowl of seventh-century type, and, finally, this mausoleum was incorporated within an urban parish church.

At Wells a Saxon burial chapel, which became incorporated within the tenth-century St Mary's Chapel east of the late Saxon cathedral, partly overlay a stone and timber mausoleum of Roman or sub-Roman date (**85**). There are also other examples of Saxon churches which incorporate the remains of Roman mausolea. At Stone-by-Faversham (Kent) a Roman mausoleum, associated with a small settlement, was utilized to form part of the chancel of a church whose nave was constructed of timber. This nave cannot be earlier than the seventh century, but obviously the mausoleum walls were then standing to a height suitable for reuse in the church structure. To what use the mausoleum had been put, if any,

85 *Wells: the surviving masonry and outline of the Roman or post-Roman mausoleum beneath St Mary's Chapel and immediately east of the site of the Saxon cathedral.*

in the intervening fifth and sixth centuries, however, we cannot tell. A further example of such a process is known from Canterbury where the church of St Martins similarly incorporates the walls of a Roman mausoleum.

Monastic enclosures

A particular characteristic of early monastic sites in the west of Britain and Ireland is the provision of a surrounding enclosure bank. This bank, usually accompanied by an external ditch, was a symbolic boundary between the sacred and the profane rather than a defensive work. According to tradition the bank was constructed by the founder of the monastery at the time of its foundation and it is known in the literature as a *vallum monasterii*. Some early examples, such as at Clonmacnois (Co. Offaly) and Iona, were rectangular in shape but most were more circular in plan. In western

Britain, *vallum* excavations have occurred on early Christian monastic sites at Iona, Glastonbury and St Helens, Isles of Scilly. Seldom has any dating evidence been recovered, but on Ardwall Island the drystone bank was thought to be original, and contemporary with the early chapels and cemeteries of sixth- to seventh-century date. At Burry Holms (Glamorgan) the earliest bank, built of turf and revetted with small stones, may have been earlier than the eleventh century.

Enclosures of this type can also be defined on some of the reused Roman temple sites in western Britain. At Uley during the late fifth or sixth century, and probably contemporary with the construction and use of the timber basilican church, a perimeter bank was built around the focal area of the site (see **83**). The core of the bank comprised a dark, fine soil, possibly the remains of turves, and was revetted by timbers which may have supported a continuous fence. The line of the bank was traced north and west of the basilica, but to the south its foundations had been destroyed by ploughing. In two places there were rectangular foundations of drystone footings and adjacent post-holes indicating the positions of complex entrances. In the reconstruction drawing (see **84**) these are shown as timber towers with gabled shingled roofs and the line of the enclosure has been projected in a curve to form a roughly oval precinct. Whether any further buildings occupied the southern and eastern sectors of this enclosure cannot be assessed owing to the severity of plough damage on the crest of the hill. The turves in the bank material must have been gathered from the vicinity for they contained large numbers of votive objects, mainly in small fragments, and late Roman coins; an assemblage which matched that found in the ritual deposits associated with the converted temple ruin.

At Lydney, the rampart of the Iron Age promontory fort, within which the Roman temple precinct had been set, was doubled in height and an outer bank was added on the north side. The make-up material contained demolition rubble from the temple settlement and was ascribed by the excavator to 'some period of recrudescent barbarism after the beginning of the fifth century'. As more recent commentators have observed, 'such an attitude to our post-Roman 'natives' is hardly acceptable today from ethical, political or historical standpoints; nor is the easy acceptance of a military explanation for the latest phases of the Lydney enclosure' (Rahtz and Watts 1979). A more likely interpretation is that the remodelled and compartmentalized temple continued in religious use well into the fifth century, and probably beyond. The refurbished bank could have functioned, if the context was Christian, as a *vallum monasterii*, and further post-Roman timber buildings may have occupied the northern sector of the enclosure, a sector which was not much investigated during the original excavation campaign. In the light of the evidence excavated at Uley, it can be suggested further that the slight and elusive remains of any timber church that might have been erected over the remains of the temple at Lydney would have been disturbed and destroyed irrevocably by the earlier excavations of 1805. At Nettleton, the 'Wick Valley bank', running south and west of the building complex, was ascribed by the excavator to the medieval period or later. However, this bank, with its collapsed drystone oolitic limestone wall and exterior ditch, may have belonged to an earlier post-Roman period.

Similarly, at Lamyatt Beacon the boundary bank and ditch which the excavator felt to be of Saxon date might have been earlier.

A further characteristic of the monastic enclosure banks is that quite often they incorporated or reused the lines of defensive banks and ditches erected in the prehistoric period. A study of the dimensions of surviving banks highlights this pattern. On sites where prehistoric earthworks were employed, as at Lydney and St Abb's head, Coldingham, the banks were in the order of 10 to 12 m (33 to 39 ft) in width, and survive to a good height. In the case of newly-built banks, however, widths of 2 to 4 m ($6\frac{1}{2}$ to 13 ft) were the norm, and this also confirms their suggested non-defensive function. Amongst the excavated examples, two sites have provided evidence for towers incorporated within the bank. Reconstructions of those at Uley are shown in **84** and a further similar foundation was excavated at Cadbury Congresbury. Again, these were not designed with defence in mind, but probably functioned to aggrandize an entrance and to symbolize the importance and power of the sacred place. This entire discussion is reminiscent of our earlier considerations of the enclosures provided for Roman temples and for the precincts of shrines in the Celtic Iron Age, and it is well known that the early Christian church of the west incorporated many Celtic traditions, not least the highly characteristic art styles and some of the pagan iconography.

Holy wells

Another traditional practice, which continued especially in Wales and Ireland, was the veneration of water at the site of springs and wells. In Wales most churches can boast a holy well close by. Often the well had Celtic connections and later came to be associated with a local Christian saint. Indeed, sometimes it was believed that the wells had been brought to life by the saints themselves. At Llangybi (Gwynedd), St Cybi is said to have struck his staff on a rock and water gushed forth, while the water of St Gwenfrewi's well (Holywell) (**86** and **colour plate 9**) is described as springing from the spot where blood fell from the severed head of the saint. Most of the surviving wells have surrounds of post-medieval date, but in a few cases foundations of enclosures or cells of drystone boulder construction remain. This is the case at St Seiriol's well on Anglesey and

at St Cybi's well, but in neither case can an early date be demonstrated. In Cornwall holy wells are also common and some were accompanied by small chapels. The earliest surviving example is the eighth- or ninth-century chapel of St Constantine at St Merryn.

The veneration of holy sources of water has survived to the present day and is illustrated dramatically by the seasonal celebrations involving 'well-dressing', practised all over the Derbyshire Peak District, for instance at Tissington. More overt are the offerings and inscriptions deposited at surviving holy wells

in remote locations, a habit which is still widespread in parts of Ireland. The nature of such offerings has been investigated in relation to one of the two holy wells associated with a ruined church dedicated to a sixth-century saint in Donegal. Close to one well was a 'cave', which is probably a natural formation of large boulders, and nearby an oval oratory or cell, also of boulders, but humanly-constructed. Around the well was a cairn of stones; among these and in the 'cave' a large number of objects have been deposited (87). The items recorded by visiting archaeologists included many glass bottles, presumably intended to contain, or to represent, the holy water and, in order of their degree of occurrence: coins, household items, Christian objects, hair accessories, fragments of clothing, small souvenirs, written tracts concerning the efficacy of holy water and many marine shells and pebbles. Such a list is highly reminiscent of the catalogues of small objects found in and around the temples of late Roman Britain.

86 *(Left) Holywell, Flintshire: the healing well of St Winifred (Gwenfrewi) is housed in an elaborate medieval structure next to the church.*

87 *(Below) Objects found within the 'cave' and around the well at Termon, Co. Donegal.*

9

The symbolism of Christianity

The beliefs of early Christians were totally at variance with those of their forbears. A single omnipotent deity was to be worshipped, private property was to be held in little account, and moral standards were set at an extremely high level. Furthermore, sacrifices of animals, let alone of fellow human beings, were expressly forbidden. But the processes of conversion and evangelism did not occur in a vacuum. Constantly the early Christians were faced with the material manifestations of pagan religion and appropriate reactions and a code of practice needed to be developed. One line of action which appeared to achieve a good degree of success was that promoted by Pope Gregory and summarized in a letter to St Augustine: 'Do not pull down the temples. Destroy the idols; purify the temples with holy water; set relics there; and let them become temples of the true God.' Thus the ancient holy places could be cleansed and refreshed, and at the same time the new religion could become embedded instantly in the minds of the newly-converted pagans, and enriched by the survival of ancestral memories. It is the absorption and adaptation of such former memories, pagan rites and symbolism by the Christian church that forms the subject matter for this final chapter.

The adaptation of actual Roman temple buildings certainly occurred and sometimes new shrines or chapels were constructed exactly over, or adjacent to, their ruined remains. Also some of these sites had been occupied in earlier times by Iron Age shrines or other places regarded as sacred by the Celts and their earlier prehistoric ancestors. In other cases where there is no evidence for veneration in either the Iron Age or Roman period, religious sites or monuments of Neolithic of Bronze Age date were enfolded within the newly enclosed Christian chapels and graveyards. We have already seen that the church at Knowlton in Dorset was built inside a surviving henge monument (**colour plate 1**) and in other instances the mounds of barrows or standing megaliths lie within the confines of Christian churchyards. The most famous example is at Rudston in Yorkshire, where the awe-inspiring megalith towers up next to the east end of the medieval church, and the place-name itself means 'rood stone'. Perhaps in early Christian times the pagan powers of the megalith had been placated by the incision of a cross, now long since worn away. Indeed it has been suggested by some scholars that the British tradition of great Anglo-Saxon standing crosses may have derived in part from the Celtic cult of menhir erection.

Foliage and water
Celtic religion embraced a special respect for nature and, in particular, the veneration of trees, sacred groves, foliage and pools or springs of water. All these aspects became absorbed into Christian symbolism and iconography (**88**). Ancient tree worship involved veneration of the tree itself and, in addition, ceremonies wherein a youth or maiden adorned and masked with leaves and branches was involved in fertility processions or festivals. The former mode of veneration survived into medieval times within the rite of maypole dancing at Maytime. These rites were performed outside the church, although often within the bounds of its surrounding graveyard. The foliage-decked fertility mummer survived as Jack-in-the-Green or the Green Man, and visual representations of

this figure, in wood or in stone, form one of the most common decorative motifs inside our medieval churches (**89**). The stylized representation is quite uniform, depicting a face mysteriously discerned through a pattern formed from the leaves growing on two branches, which stem from the mouth. The leaves represented are usually those of the oak, a tree which was sacred to the Celts. The traditional ceremony of the Green Man involved a man whose head and shoulders were covered by a wicker cage thickly woven with leaves and in Europe wicker giants were filled sometimes with live animals. This immediately recalls the wicker figures filled with human victims that were described so graphically by Caesar.

Water was quoted throughout the New Testament as a symbol of purification, spiritual refreshment and of life itself. In a liturgical context it was associated with the cleansing of ritual vessels in the Eucharist and in the very important rite of baptism. A wine container (*cantharus*), perhaps associated with the Eucharist, became one of the symbols employed by the early Christians (**90**). Not surprisingly,

88 *Carved foliage at Wells Cathedral.*

as seen in the last chapter, many wells and springs traditionally associated with Celtic deities were taken over and ascribed to Christian saints. From early times Christians have employed depictions of animals and birds as religious symbols and, once again, this may be seen as a characteristic of native tradition. Medieval church art included depictions of the animals employed by the earliest Christians in the Roman world, such as the fish, the dolphin (**91**), doves and the peacock alongside many others: the lion, symbol of goodness; the panther as a sign of the Resurrection; and mythical beasts reminiscent of the curvilinear monsters found throughout Celtic art. Interestingly, the most pervasive artistic device employed to symbolize Christ himself was a gentle, domestic animal, the *Agnus Dei*, Lamb of God.

The cult of saints
One very specific aspect of Christianity which appears to possess some firm native, and originally pagan, roots is the rise of the cult of

saints and the veneration of relics. This cult originated in the fourth century and rapidly spread throughout the world of late antiquity. Cults connected with the early martyrs of Rome were becoming well known by the fourth century in areas north of the Alps, and during the fourth and fifth centuries the bodies of many local Gaulish and Germanic holy men and women also became the subjects for veneration. The Christian cult of saints involved the digging up and dismemberment of bodies, the selection of body parts, and their translation to locations where they were accessible to the living. In other words the bodies, or pieces of them, were translated from grave to church and, often, from suburban cemetery to urban cathedral. For instance, in Milan, Ambrose appropriated the relics of St Verbaius and St Protasius, which had been discovered in 385, and displayed them within his new basilica. Further north, the sites of saints' graves often became the *foci* for the development of early Christian churches outside Roman towns, although sometimes the holy remains were moved to more central locations within the walls. Owing to the paucity of appropriate material or literary evidence, little attention has been paid to the nature of the saintly relics themselves and it is only for the Anglo-Saxon period in England that we begin to gain any

insight into topics such as the mechanics of translation, the selection of particular body parts as relics, gender representation amongst the chosen individuals, or the archaeology of the associated non-corporeal relics as well as the ingenious containers devised for their protection.

The identification of the exact body parts extracted for translation has been of little interest to historians, either ancient or modern, and material remains from the Anglo-Saxon or late Roman periods are few indeed. However, cursory examination of relics and reliquaries during visits to continental Europe suggests that, at least in medieval times, the body parts most commonly selected for particular veneration were the heart, samples of blood, pieces of skull, complete or fragmentary limb bones and the small components of hands or fingers. To dismember a body, however holy, was of course at total variance with primary Christian beliefs which stated that the dead human body should remain inviolate in preparation for the Second Coming. Thus certain high-principled popes, such as Gregory the Great, were strongly opposed to the fragmentation of saints' remains. Such restrictions led to the promotion and widespread use of the secondary or non-corporeal relics which became commonplace within early medieval Europe and Anglo-Saxon England. These included items such as objects owned by the saint in question, water within which the bones had been washed at the time of ritual translation, fragments of apparel, earth

89 *Green Man carved on a late medieval bench-end in the church at Crowcombe, Somerset.*

90 Cantharus: *the central motif of a mosaic from the Fifehead Neville villa.*

91 *Representation of a dolphin from the Fifehead Neville mosaic.*

soaked by martyrial blood or even fragments of fabric which had been in contact with the saintly remains themselves. However, if the saint's body were to be dismembered by pagan enemies, then chosen parts could be given full ritual treatment, even in Anglo-Saxon England. Thus Oswald was killed in battle by Penda of Mercia, and his severed head and arms were erected on a stake on the battlefield. Subsequently the decapitated body was taken to Bardney, now in Lincolnshire, but the head

92 *The Monymusk reliquary, made in the shape of a house from wood with gilt and silver ornaments, may once have contained a relic of St Columba (105 mm (4 in) wide).*

was transported to Lindisfarne, while his right arm was carried to Bamburgh (Northumberland) where it came to be encased in silver.

Individual bones were sometimes employed in cures, such as in the case of a paralysed monk being cured by contact with some saintly hand-bones. It is interesting to note once again the supremacy of head, arm and hand bones. In the absence of any contemporary lists detailing fourth-century or early medieval saints it is difficult to estimate the relative incidence of male and female candidates. However, the fourth-century calendar of Rome can be reconstructed from various later, and rather unsatisfactory, sources. These lists of saints' and feast days show that most of the saints, perhaps as

many as 90 per cent, were male, but that women were significantly represented from the beginning.

The process of canonization was closely linked to the act of translation, an act of such importance that it was often commemorated by a feast day separate from that of the martyrdom or death of the saint. Translation usually involved the transference of corporeal remains from the original grave to the interior of a church. The remains were there deposited above ground within a specially designed coffin-reliquary or tomb, usually in or near to the site of the altar. Here the remains could be viewed and venerated and, in time, elaborate shrines or other embellishments could easily be accommodated. Such shrines and coffin-reliquaries were often adorned with religious carvings, sculptured detail and precious stones, and many were modelled in the shape of a miniature house, or church, characterized by a ridged roof, represented in stone or wood (**92**). The essence of the shrine or reliquary was its enclosed nature. The holy relics were either hidden totally from view or could be glimpsed but dimly through narrow slits or windows (**93**). This element of secrecy and mystery was developed further in the early medieval period by the employment within churches of corridor crypts, through which access to saintly tombs and relics, installed beneath the high altar, were controlled by the priests and guardians. Originating probably at the shrine of St Peter in Rome, the popularity of such crypts spread quickly through Europe and is well exemplified in England by the Saxon examples at Brixworth (Northants.), Ripon (Yorkshire) and Repton (Derbyshire). The dark and narrow secret passages would have inspired feelings of awe, fear and mystery within the believers who approached the saintly tomb. No doubt these feelings would have been intensified with ingenious methods of lighting and sources of fragrance positioned at the tomb itself.

Recent scholars have attempted to link the expansion of the cult of saints in the late fourth century to contemporary social and political pressures. Thus the cult was strongly promoted by the bishops and the ruling classes of the Roman empire, in order to enhance their own status and power. Like Ambrose at Milan, many church and secular leaders appropriated relics, translated them to new churches within their expanding urban centres and manipulated their availability to the community at large. All this was linked to the growing wealth of the church, and to the increasing importance of urban life. The cult of saints reflected the greater influence of individuals and the desire for personal security and power. A similar theory linking power politics and the cult of the saints may be applied in the case of Anglo-Saxon England, where the Lives of Saints were addressed mainly to the ecclesiastical world and where secular involvement was limited to those of noble or royal birth. Indeed, many saintly cults were centred on royal churches and the cults were promoted by the royal house. Thus the early cult of saints may be seen to have been orchestrated by the members of religious and other high-ranking elites, and closely linked to the demonstration of honourable descent down from the holiest of ancestors.

Whilst such an analysis can provide a convincing explanation for the rise and spread of the cult of the saints during the fourth to seventh centuries, the development of the cult in medieval times and, in particular, the widespread depiction of saints in ecclesiastical art, may owe its origins to something more basic. Thus the veneration of a series of very holy persons, whilst retaining doctrinal respectability, could mimic the pagan beliefs which embraced a whole pantheon of gods and goddesses. At the same time a feminine dimension could be introduced to a religion which had become dominated by male leaders, not least by the very successful cult of the Virgin Mary, mother of God and archetypal earth-mother. None of this would have been acceptable to the Christians of the first century, but the cults did seem to fulfil some very deep-seated human requirement.

Emblems and ritual

Within the stained glass windows and on the painted walls of medieval churches the predominantly illiterate congregations could 'read' stories from the Old and New Testaments and identify early martyrs and their favourite patron saints. To aid understanding, each individual portrayed bore a symbol, just as the Roman and pre-Roman deities had in the art forms of previous eras. The symbols allotted to the Christian saints were usually small material objects which could be held in the hand, while those associated with Roman gods and goddesses also included objects from nature, such as the sun or moon, and animal attributes (**94**). The Christian symbols

usually referred to the profession of an apostle or the means of martyrdom in the case of martyrs. Thus St Catherine holds the spiked wheel which was the instrument of her torture and St Lawrence the gridiron upon which he was roasted. James the Greater, reputed to have spread the gospel to Spain, is shown wearing a pilgrim's habit, while Matthew the tax collector carries a money-bag or box. Later, certain saints became adopted as patrons for different groups of tradesmen and the symbols of their former death and torture became devices set in the sphere of commerce. For instance, St Bartholomew who holds the knife with which he was flayed was adopted as the patron of tanners in the medieval period. All of this appears to possess a very pagan flavour and can be contrasted with the stark symbolism

93 *At Whitchurch Canonicorum, Dorset, the stone shrine of St White is pierced by three oval holes through which pilgrims might have glimpsed or touched the relics or dust of the saint. Today the holes are still used for the deposition of requests or prayers recorded on postcards.*

94 *Personal attributes in Christian and Roman iconography.*

for Christ himself embodied in the gospels. Amongst the symbols invoked in the 'Seven Sayings' of St John's Gospel there are only two material symbols, and these are the very special symbols of the Eucharist, representing the body of Christ himself: 'I am the bread of life' (John 6:35) and 'I am the true vine' (John 15:1). The other symbols are abstract, personal and unique: 'I am the Light of the World' (John 8:12); 'I am the door of the sheepfold' (John 10:7); 'I am the good shepherd' (John 10:11); 'I am the resurrection and the life' (John 11:25) and 'I am the way, the truth and the life' (John 14:6).

Christian ceremonies

Most religions include elements of ritual and worship which incorporate prayer, sacrifice and ceremonial. From the very beginning, Christianity included the citation and singing of prayers and hymns, a custom which was modelled directly on Jewish practice. The earliest surviving full description of a Eucharistic service dates to the second century and outlines a sequence of events which is not dissimilar to the modern liturgy. The aim of the Eucharist was to remind believers of the death of Christ and to reinforce the promise of eternal life. The supernatural powers of the Eucharist displayed magical overtones (bread turns to flesh; wine

CHRISTIAN		ROMAN	
Saint	*Symbol*	*God/Goddess*	*Attribute*
Peter	keys	Mercury	cock, ram/goat, money bag
Andrew	saltire cross	Cupid	arrow
James the Greater	pilgrim's habit	Hercules	club
John	dragon in chalice	Mars	weapons, horse, goose
Thomas	spear	Minerva	helmet
James Minor	club	Apollo	sun
Philip	loaves or tall cross	Ceres	corn
Bartholomew	flaying knife	Bacchus	wine, grapes
Matthew	money-bag or box	Jupiter	wheel, dolphin, bull
Simon	fish, oar or sword	Silvanus	stag
Jude	boat	Diana	dog
Mathias	halberd	Cernunnos	stag-horns
Paul	sword	Vulcan	hammer
John the Baptist	*Agnus Dei* on book	Luna	moon
Catherine	spiked wheel		
Barbara	small tower		
George	dragon		
Lawrence	gridiron		
Christopher	Christ on shoulder		
Edward	ring		

becomes blood) and from very early on it was perceived as a sacrificial act; the service did not embody the sacrifice but it served to honour it. The sacrifice offered by the death of Christ happened 'once and for all', but was to be commemorated in ritual terms on a regular basis, and at his specific request. The sacrificial context was promoted by Paul: 'God presented him (Christ) as a sacrifice of atonement...' (Romans 3:25), and the writer of the letter to the Hebrews: 'Then Christ would have had to suffer many times since the creation of the world. But now he has appeared once for all at the end of the ages to do away with sin by the sacrifice of himself' (Hebrews 9:26–7). However, the word 'sacrifice' does not appear in the recorded sayings of Christ himself, except within quotations from the psalms.

At first the gatherings of early Christians involved little ceremonial but as the centuries

passed a priesthood developed, the involvement of women became prescribed and downgraded, monasticism evolved and ceremonial became more elaborate. The sacred rites of baptism and the Eucharist became enmeshed in the trappings of complex preparatory rituals, vigils and fastings, secret incantations and repeated anointings. Such developments were at variance with much of the doctrine and guidelines provided in the gospels and many beliefs and practices appear to have been absorbed from the pagan surroundings and the pre-Christian past. However, it is fairly certain that it was these timely adaptations and embellishments that allowed the Church to survive and flourish through the fourth and fifth centuries.

The objects associated with baptismal and Eucharistic rites are mainly vessels: fonts of stone, lead or marble and the wine and water jars, paten and chalice that became essential equipment for celebration of the Eucharist. Early surviving fonts are usually of eleventh- or twelfth-century date, and are often plain. The absence of any surviving stone fonts of pre-tenth century date indicates either that the necessary tanks were tubs made from wood, or that baptism took place in rivers or pools during open-air gatherings. It has further been suggested that sometimes such gatherings may have occurred at periodic fairs or markets, held on sites which in some cases had been used for communal purposes since prehistoric times.

Decorated examples of early fonts include those depicting biblical scenes or miracles of the saints, inextricably entwined with the tendrils, scrolls and monsters of the native Celtic tradition (95). The human head is conspicuous in such medieval art styles and often occurs in areas connected with water; above holy water stoups and around the bowls of carved stone fonts. The flowering of metalworking around the Irish Sea from the fifth to seventh centuries displayed a remarkable juxtapositioning of native Celtic design and Christian symbolism. Many objects were manufactured in the monastic workshops of Ireland and were destined for ecclesiastical use. The Ardagh Chalice, made around AD 700, was composed of silver sheet. The handles, attachment plaques and medallions were decorated in gold filigree patterns and inlaid with red and blue enamels, and further embellishment was provided by glass beads and studs. In contrast to this rich, but abstract, adornment, the names of the twelve apostles and some interlace was lightly engraved upon the body of the vessel. Cups, bowls and a strainer, all suitable for use in preparation of the Eucharist were present in the late Roman silver hoard from Mildenhall, and with them was a series of triangular silver plaques. In shape and style these match the votive leaves and feathers found on many a Roman temple site. Those from Water Newton were fashioned in precious metal and many were embellished with prominent chi-rho motifs (colour plate 10). The modification of pagan ideology for Christian consumption was almost as old as Christianity itself.

95 *Carved stone font in the church of St Michael, Castle Frome (Herefordshire). The design included signs of the Evangelists between zones of interlace and plaiting, and three powerful crouching figures at the base. Probably twelfth century AD.*

Appendix

List of sites

Site	County	Excavator(s)	Publication reference
			(see Bibliography)
			(fc = forthcoming)

Iron Age shrines and cemeteries

Danebury	Hants	Professor B. Cunliffe	1984
Winnall Down	Hants	P. Fasham	1985
Poundbury	Dorset	C. Sparey Green	Farwell and Molleson fc

Roman temples over Iron Age shrines

Lydney	Glos	Sir R. E. M. Wheeler	1932
Maiden Castle	Dorset	Sir R. E. M. Wheeler	1943
South Cadbury	Somerset	Professor L. Alcock	1972
Uley	Glos	A. Ellison (Woodward)	1980 and fc
Lancing Ring	Sussex	O. Bedwin	1981
Harlow	Essex	N. France and B. Gobel	1985
Woodeaton	Oxon	R. Goodchild and J. Kirk	1955; 1949
Brigstock	Northants	E. Greenfield and M. Taylor	1963
Hayling Island	Hants	G. Soffe, A. King and the late R. Downey	1980 and fc
Bath	Avon	Professor B. Cunliffe and P. Davenport	1985

Roman temples associated with cemeteries and/or an early church

Brean Down	Somerset	A. ApSimon	1965
Nettleton Scrubb	Wilts	W. Wedlake	1982
Icklingham	Suffolk	S. West and J. Plouviez	1976
Lamyatt Beacon	Somerset	R. Leech	1986
Henley Wood	Avon	E. Greenfield	L. Watts and P. Leach fc
Witham	Essex	R. Turner	1982
Uley	Glos	(see above)	1980 and fc

Unassociated temples

Collyweston	Northants	G. Knocker	1966
Pagans Hill	Avon	Professor P. Rahtz	1951; Rahtz and Harris 1957
Coleshill	Warwicks	J. Magilton	1980

continued overleaf

Site	County	Excavator(s)	Publication reference
Late Roman or post-Roman cemeteries and churches			
Poundbury	Dorset	(see above)	Farwell and Molleson, fc
Colchester	Essex	P. Crummy	1980 and 1990
Wells	Somerset	W. Rodwell	1982
Cannington	Somerset	Professor P. Rahtz	fc
Lullingstone	Kent	G. Meates	1979
Lankhills	Hants	G. Clarke	1979
Cirencester	Glos	A. McWhirr, L. Viner and the late C. Wells	1982
Ilchester/Northover	Somerset	P. Leach	1982 and fc
Richborough	Kent	J. Bushe-Fox	Brown 1971
Silchester	Hants	I. Richmond	Frere 1975; King 1983
Littlecote	Wilts	B. Walters	fc

Places to visit

Most of the sites listed were rescued by excavation in advance of development. Many are thus destroyed and so nothing is left to see.

Hillforts

Several of the hillforts that contained shrines can be visited, although only at Maiden Castle are the remains of temple foundations laid out for view.

Maiden Castle Short, steep walk from English Heritage car park to the western entrance.

Danebury Easy access from Hampshire County Council car park and picnic area.

South Cadbury A steep walk from the eastern side; take the lane next to South Cadbury church.

Roman villas

Littlecote The triconch building with restored mosaic floors. In the grounds of Littlecote Manor, west of Hungerford.

Lullingstone The estate chapel. An English Heritage site, south-east of Eynsford.

Temples and early churches in towns

Bath The Roman baths adjacent to the temple precinct and associated museum.

Colchester The Butt Road church, laid out next to the new police station.

Lincoln St-Paul-in-the-Bail early church plan, within the courtyard of the former Roman forum, now marked out in granite sets.

London The temple of Mithras, Walbrook.

Museum collections

The British Museum has a magnificent collection of religious material including the finds from Uley, the Water Newton treasure and the mosaic from Hinton St Mary. Other museums worth a visit are those at Bath, the Ashmolean Museum, Oxford (finds from Woodeaton), the Dorset County Museum at Dorchester (Maiden Castle) and Harlow Museum.

Further reading

A list of the 32 key sites discussed throughout this book may be found in the Appendix (p. 135). This also supplies author references which are arranged alphabetically in the Bibliography.

1 The placing of shrines

The best general study covering Iron Age shrines and Roman temples is that edited by Rodwell (1980). Wilson (1973) and Blagg (1986) have supplied specific analyses of types of location, while the classical sources have been considered in detail by Wait (1985). Recent summaries of Bronze Age barrows and the henge monuments have been supplied by Grinsell (1979) and Wainwright (1990) respectively.

2 The structure of shrines

Useful summaries of the evidence for Iron Age shrines may be found in Piggott (1968), Wait (1985) and Drury (1980). The classic study of Romano-Celtic architecture for Britain is Lewis (1966), while more recent theories and data are highlighted in Rodwell (1980). The reconstructions for the Uley temple were developed in conjunction with Dr Warwick Rodwell.

3 Belief and ritual

The Iron Age background is covered well by Collis (1984), Piggott (1968), Ross (1970) and Wait (1985). Henig (1984) provides an extremely useful commentary on religion in Roman Britain, while details of objects and specific cults may be found in Green (1976) and Ross (1967). The reuse of religious objects has been discussed by Merrifield (1987, Chapter 4).

4 Offerings and sacrifice

No general studies exist and detail must be sought in individual site reports. The subject of sacrifice is considered by Piggott (1968), Wait (1985, Chapters 4 and 5) and Henig (1984).

5 Burials and cemeteries

Analysis of Iron Age burial rites is supplied by Whimster (1981), Wait (1985, Chapter 4) and, for Danebury, Walker (1984). No general summary of the Roman material exists but a useful introduction is provided by Reece (1977). The Christian candidates are discussed by Thomas (1981, Chapter 9).

6 The Roman church

The key study is Thomas (1981); for further information see Henig (1984, Chapter 10) and Rodwell and Bentley (1984, Chapter 1). The Dorset mosaics are illustrated in RCHM *Dorset*, Vols. I and III.

7 The early Christian church

General studies include Thomas (1971a and 1971b), Morris (1983) and, for summaries of specific sites, Laing (1975). The Welsh material has been brought together by Victory (1977). The description of the modern well deposits in Donegal is taken from Rahtz and Watts 1979, Appendix II. The interpretation of the basilica at Uley incorporates the unpublished views of Dr Warwick Rodwell and Professor Philip Rahtz; a possible early date for the Wick Valley bank at Nettleton was first advanced by Richard Kemp.

8 The symbolism of Christianity

Anderson (1971) provides an elegant overview of Christian imagery and the absorption of pagan ideas. The cult of saints has been analysed for Europe and Anglo-Saxon England by Brown (1981) and Rollason (1990) respectively. For a new interpretation of baptismal places, see Morris (1991). A useful summary of the development of early Christianity is that supplied by Walsh (1986); for a mass of exciting detail see Lane Fox (1986).

Bibliography

Alcock, L. (1972), 'By South Cadbury is that Camelot...' The Excavation of Cadbury Castle 1966–1970, Thames and Hudson, London.

Anderson, M. D. (1971), History and Imagery in British Churches, John Murray, London.

ApSimon, A. M. (1965), 'The Roman Temple on Brean Down, Somerset', Proceedings University Bristol Spelaeological Society 10, No. 3, 195–258.

Bedwin, O. (1981), 'Excavations at Lancing Down, West Sussex 1980', Sussex Archaeol. Colls. 119, 37–56.

Blagg, T. (1986), 'Roman religious sites in the British landscape', Landscape History 8, 16–24.

Brown, P.D.C. (1971), 'The church at Richborough', Britannia II, 225–31.

Brown, P. (1981), The Cult of Saints: Its Rise and Function in Latin Christianity, SCM, Chicago and London.

Clarke, G. (1979), Pre-Roman and Roman Winchester Part II. The Roman Cemetery at Lankhills, Oxford University Press.

Collis, J. (1984), The European Iron Age, Batsford, London.

Crummy, P. (1980), 'The Temples of Roman Colchester', in Rodwell (ed.) (1980), 243–84.

Crummy, P. (1990), 'A Roman church in Colchester', Current Archaeology No.120, 406–8.

Cunliffe, B. W. (1984), Danebury: an Iron Age Hillfort in Hampshire. Vol. I: The excavations 1969–1978: the site. Vol. II: the finds. London. Council for British Archaeology Research Report 52.

Cunliffe, B. and Davenport, P. (1985), The Temple of Sulis Minerva at Bath. Vol. 1 (1) The Site. Oxford.

Downey, R., King, A. and Soffe, G. (1980), 'The Hayling Island Temple and Religious Connections across the Channel', in Rodwell (ed.) (1980), 289–304.

Drury, P. J. (1980), 'Non-Classical Religious Buildings in Iron Age and Roman Britain: A Review', in Rodwell (ed.) (1980), 45–78.

Farwell, D. and Molleson, T. (forthcoming) Poundbury Volume II: The Cemeteries. Excavations 1964–1987, Dorset Nat. Hist. and Archaeol. Soc. monograph.

Fasham, P.J. (1985), The Prehistoric Settlement at Winnall Down, Winchester. Hants Field Club Monograph 2, Winchester.

France, N.E. and Gobel, B.M. (1985), The Romano-British Temple at Harlow, Alan Sutton, Gloucester.

Frere, S. S. (1975), 'The Silchester Church: The Excavation by Sir Ian Richmond in 1961', Archaeologia 105, 277–302.

Goodchild, R. and Kirk, J. R. (1955), 'The Romano-Celtic Temple at Woodeaton', Oxoniensia XIX, 15–37.

Green, M. J. (1976), The Religions of Civilian Roman Britain, BAR 24, Oxford.

Greenfield, E. and Taylor M. V. (1963), 'The Romano-British Shrines at Brigstock, Northants.', Antiquaries Journal 43, 228–63.

Grinsell, L.V. (1979), Barrows in England and Wales, Shire Archaeology No. 8, Princes Risborough.

Henig, M. (1984), Religion in Roman Britain, Batsford, London.

King, A. (1983), 'The Roman Church at Silchester Reconsidered', Oxford Journal of Archaeology Vol. 2, no. 2, 225–38.

Kirk, J. R. (1949), 'Bronzes from Woodeaton, Oxon', Oxoniensia XIV, 1–45.

Knocker, G. M. (1966), 'Excavations in Collyweston Great Wood, Northamptonshire', Archaeological Journal CXXII, 52–72.

Laing, L. (1975), The Archaeology of Late Celtic Britain and Ireland c.400–1200 AD, Methuen, London.

Lane Fox, R. (1986), Pagans and Christians in the Mediterranean world from the second century AD to the conversion of Constantine, Viking Penguin, London.

Leach, P. J. (1982), Ilchester Volume I. Excavations 1974–75, Western Archaeological Trust, Bristol.

Leach, P. J. (forthcoming), 'The evaluation of a late Roman cemetery in the gardens of Northover House, Ilchester', in Ilchester Volume 2, Sheffield.

Leech, R. (1986), 'The Excavation of a Romano-Celtic Temple and a Later Cemetery on Lamyatt Beacon, Somerset', Britannia XVII, 259–328.

Lewis, M. J. T. (1966), Temples in Roman Britain, Cambridge University Press.

Magilton, J. R. (1980), 'The Church of St Helen-on-the-Walls, Aldwark', *The Archaeology of York,* 10/1.

Meates, G. W. (1979), *The Roman Villa at Lullingstone, Kent. Vol. 1: The Site*, Kent Archaeol. Soc.

McWhirr, A., Viner, L. and Wells, C. (1982), *Cirencester Excavations II: Romano-British Cemeteries at Cirencester*, Cirencester Excavation Committee.

Merrifield, R. (1987), *The Archaeology of Ritual and Magic,* Batsford, London.

Morris, R. (1983), *The Church in British Archaeology,* CBA Res. Rep., 47, London.

Morris, R. (1991) 'Baptismal Places: 600–800. In *Peoples and Places in northern Europe 500–1600. Essays in Honour of Peter Hayes Sawyer,* eds. I. Wood and N. Lund, Boydell Press, Woodbridge, 15–24.

Piggott, S. (1968), *The Druids*, Thames and Hudson, London.

Rahtz, P. A. (1951), 'The Roman Temple at Pagans Hill, Chew Stoke, N. Somerset', *Proc. Somerset Arch. and Nat. Hist. Soc.* 96, 112–42.

Rahtz, P. A. and Harris, L. G. (1957), 'The Temple Well and other Buildings at Pagan's Hill, Chew Stoke, N. Somerset', *Proc. Somerset Arch. and Nat. Hist. Soc.*, 101/2, 15–51.

Rahtz, P. A. and Watts, L. (1979), 'The End of Roman Temples in the West of Britain', in Casey, P. J. (ed.), *The End of Roman Britain,* BAR 71, Oxford, 183–210.

Rahtz, P. A. *et alia* (forthcoming), *Excavation of a late Roman and post-Roman cemetery at Cannington, Somerset.*

Reece, R. (ed) (1977), *Burial in the Roman World,* CBA Res. Rep. 22, London.

Rodwell, W. J. (ed.) (1980), *Temples, Churches and Religion in Roman Britain,* BAR 77, Oxford.

Rodwell, W. (1982), 'From mausoleum to minster: the early development of Wells Cathedral', in S.M. Pearce (ed.), *The Early Church in Western Britain and Ireland,* BAR 102, Oxford, 49–59.

Rodwell, W. and Bentley, J. (1984), *Our Christian Heritage,* London.

Rollason, D. (1990), *Saints and Relics in Anglo-Saxon England,* Blackwell, Oxford.

Ross, A. (1967), *Pagan Celtic Britain*, Routledge and Kegan Paul, London.

Ross, A. (1970), *Everyday Life of the Pagan Celts,* Batsford, London.

Thomas, C. (1971a), *The Early Christian Archaeology of North Britain,* Oxford University Press.

Thomas, C. (1971b), *Britain and Ireland in Early Christian Times AD 400–800,* Thames and Hudson, London.

Thomas, C. (1981), *Christianity in Roman Britain to AD 500,* Batsford, London.

Turner, R. (1982), *Ivy Chimneys, Witham. An Interim Report,* Chelmsford.

Victory, S. (1977), *The Celtic Church in Wales,* SPCK, London.

Wait, G.A. (1985), *Ritual and Religion in Iron Age Britain,* BAR, 149, Oxford.

Wainwright, G.J. (1990), *The Henge Monuments,* Thames and Hudson, London.

Walker, L. (1984), 'The deposition of the human remains', in Cunliffe (1984), 442–62.

Walsh, M. (1986), *Roots of Christianity*, Grafton, London.

Walters, B. and Phillips, B. (n.d.), *Archaeological Excavations in Littlecote Park Wiltshire 1979 and 1980*, Littlecote.

Watts, L. and Leach, P. J. (forthcoming), *Henley Wood: the Romano-British temples and a post-Roman cemetery; excavations by E. Greenfield and others between 1960 and 1968.* CBA Research Report.

Wedlake, W. J. (1982), *The Excavation of the Shrine at Apollo at Nettleton, Wiltshire, 1956–1971*, Soc. Ant. Res. Rep. XL, London.

West, S. C. and Plouviez, J. (1976), 'The Roman Site at Icklingham', *East Anglian Archaeol.* 3, 63–126.

Wheeler, R. E. M. (1943), *Maiden Castle, Dorset,* Soc. Ant. Res. Rep. XII, London.

Wheeler, R. E. M. and Wheeler, T. V. (1932), *Report on the excavation of the prehistoric, Roman and post-Roman site in Lydney Park, Gloucestershire*, Soc. Ant. Research Rpt. IX, Oxford.

Whimster, R. (1981), *Burial Practices in Iron Age Britain*, BAR 90, Oxford.

Wilson, D. R. (1973), 'Temples in Britain: a topographical survey', *Caesarodunum* No. 8, 24–44, Tours.

Woodward, A. B. and Leach, P. J. (forthcoming), *The Uley Shrines. Excavation of a Ritual Complex on West Hill, Uley, Gloucestershire: 1977–9,* HBMC Monograph, London.

Glossary

abaton Building at a healing shrine within which pilgrims retired for ritual periods of sleeping. During each sleep supernatural healing or prophetic dreams might be experienced.

apse Semicircular or polygonal extension, usually in a church.

caduceus The symbolic emblem carried by Mercury, usually represented as a pair of serpents twined around a wand.

cella Central space or room within a temple.

clerestory The part of the wall of a church above the aisle roofs and pierced by a series of windows.

martyrium Chapel or shrine erected in memory of a martyr.

memoria Monument or chapel dedicated to the memory of a particular individual.

menhir A large standing stone erected as a monument.

millefiori Ornamental glass formed from rods of differing colours and sizes, fused together and cut into horizontal sections.

narthex Western porch or anteroom in a church, originally designed for women or converts under instruction.

nemeton (Greek) A sacred grove

nymphaeum Shrine dedicated to nymphs, semi-divine beings associated with water, fountains or trees.

patera Flat dish or saucer used for pouring libations as sacrifices.

piscina Holy water stoup, often found just inside the door of a church.

podium Artificial platform for a temple.

reliquary A small shrine, casket or other container within which a relic or relics are housed.

repoussé Technique of decorating metal objects whereby a design is formed in relief by hammering from the reverse surface.

soakaway Pit, often filled with rubble, designed for the drainage of waste water.

strap-end Metal terminal hammered on to the end of a leather or fabric strap; often decorated.

stylus Pointed Roman implement used for writing on wax or lead tablets.

temenos The sacred precinct or enclosure around a temple, usually defined by a wall or a ditch.

tholos A circular, domed building.

totemism The employment of an animal, or other natural object, as an emblem and a symbolic ancestor for a human social group.

translation The movement of the body or remains of a saint from the primary grave to a shrine, church or martyrium.

voussoir Tapered stone forming part of an arch or vault.

Index